Praise for *The Way to Brave*

I don't know a soul on the planet who couldn't use some courage. Andy will help you discover a fresh supply. Read it bravely.

JOHN ORTBERG
Senior Pastor of Menlo Church; author of *Soul Keeping*

I've known Andy McQuitty as a friend and spiritual mentor for years; I often look to him for the tools to live courageously in difficult times. In our modern world, it is more difficult than ever to find the strength to overcome the Goliaths all around us. Let us all look to David as an example of God's limitless power, and use Andy's book as a powerful tool to become faithful disciples of Jesus Christ.

MARK TEIXEIRA
Entrepreneur, TV analyst, philanthropist, and former three-time MLB All-Star first baseman

In an age of ever-increasing hostility toward those who dare to actually take Jesus and the Bible seriously, Andy McQuitty shows us what it takes to courageously infiltrate and impact the culture and world God has placed us in. After all, we aren't here by mistake. We're here on special assignment.

LARRY OSBORNE
Pastor and Author, North Coast Church

Andy McQuitty hits the nail on the head when he notes that "the American public square no longer honors fundamental Christian values . . . Sincere believers aren't emulated and admired. They're scapegoated and ridiculed by our culture's top four opinion-shaping institutions." So what are we as believers to do? In these tumultuous times, we must move forward with boldness—yet in a spirit of love. Just as God prepared David for his Goliath world, He wants to shape us, too. Andy takes us through five key areas that will help equip us to "fight the good fight" while making a positive impact on our neighbors.

JAMES ROBISON
Founder and president, LIFE Outreach International, Fort Worth, TX

Now more than ever, we live in a broken world and th~ ~~~~~
succeed in these times we are living in, w
against common culture and take on Gol
for the battles that lie ahead.

JUSTIN LEONARD
Golf analyst and 12-time PGA Tour winn

Far more than a how-to book, in *The Way to Brave*, Andy introduces us to five foundational divine acts upon which the Spirit builds David-like courage to face Goliath-sized giants. With well-told inspirational stories from his own life, his church, and history (especially the Celts), Andy makes biblical truth come alive. More than one well-chosen quote made me pause to think, feel, and be freshly filled with divine courage. Read it and share it, because in this chaotic world, we need more men and women of spiritual courage.

BRUCE B. MILLER
Author, *Your Life in Rhythm*, and other titles

The Way to Brave is indeed the need of the time we live in now. In this new book Andy shares the path that believers, who can be doorkeepers and peaceable warriors, need to follow in a culture that does not have their interests at heart. It's time to make a plan and plant a garden. Learn what that looks like practically in this fresh new volume.

DAVE TRAVIS
CEO Leadership Network

In *The Way to Brave*, my dear friend Pastor Andy tells us about the kind of courage-inducing community that Heather and I experienced at Irving Bible Church during the twelve years we lived in Dallas and attended IBC. Through the teaching of Andy and the community at IBC, we were both encouraged to stand strong and be a light for Jesus on the PGA Tour and in various efforts to fight the evil of sex trafficking. I recommend you read this book if you too would like to be inspired on how to walk in the way to brave.

BEN CRANE
5-time winner on PGA Tour

Wow! What a great book! It's great encouragement for Jesus followers who are looking to remain faithful (or become more so) in post-Christian America. But it's also the kind of book you can hand to your friends who are not yet Jesus followers. The book's message is profoundly relevant to all of us immersed in the current culture of anxiety. In *The Way to Brave*, Andy's depth and range as soul-curator rises to a new level.

REGGIE MCNEAL
Leadership consultant and bestselling author, *Kingdom Come* and *Kingdom Collaborators*

Billy Graham famously obseverd, "Courage is contagious. When a brave man takes a stand, the spines of others are often stiffened". If you need your spine stiffened spend some time with Andy in these pages as he remembers one of the greatest stands of faith in history. The way to brave is to follow others, like David, who courageously model what it means to trust God's call, walk in God's provision, develop a Godly character, prove their faith, and put into practice what they say they believe. Read on and be stiffened.

TODD WAGNER
Pastor, Watermark Community Church
Author of *Come and See*

THE
WAY
TO BRAVE

SHAPING A DAVID FAITH
FOR TODAY'S GOLIATH WORLD

ANDY McQUITTY

MOODY PUBLISHERS
CHICAGO

Unless otherwise noted, Scripture quotations are taken from the Holy Bible, New International Version®, NIV®. Copyright © 1973, 1978, 1984, 2011 by Biblica, Inc.™ Used by permission of Zondervan. All rights reserved worldwide. www.zondervan.com The "NIV" and "New International Version" are trademarks registered in the United States Patent and Trademark Office by Biblica, Inc.™

Scripture quotations marked ESV are from The Holy Bible, English Standard Version® (ESV®), copyright © 2001 by Crossway, a publishing ministry of Good News Publishers. Used by permission. All rights reserved.

Scripture quotations marked KJV are taken from the King James Version.

Scripture quotations marked MSG are from The Message, copyright © by Eugene H. Peterson 1993, 1994, 1995, 1996, 2000, 2001, 2002. Used by permission of Tyndale House Publishers, Inc.

Scripture quotations marked NASB are taken from the New American Standard Bible®, Copyright © 1960, 1962, 1963, 1968, 1971, 1972, 1973, 1975, 1977, 1995 by The Lockman Foundation. Used by permission. (www.Lockman.org).

Scripture quotations marked NKJV are taken from the New King James Version. Copyright © 1982 by Thomas Nelson. Used by permission. All rights reserved.

All emphasis in Scripture has been added.

Edited by Connor Sterchi and Jeremiah Betron
Interior Design: Ragont Design
Author photo: Hansel Dodds/Hansel Photography
Cover Design: Erik M. Peterson
Cover illustration of city skyline copyright © 2014 by Bakal/iStock (517266871). All rights reserved.
Cover illustrations of David and Goliath copyright © 2017 by Andrey/Lightstock (258392). All rights reserved.

Library of Congress Cataloging-in-Publication Data

Names: McQuitty, Eric A. (Eric Andrew), author.
Title: The way to brave : shaping a David faith for today's Goliath world / Andy McQuitty.
Description: Chicago : Moody Publishers, 2018. | Includes bibliographical references.
Identifiers: LCCN 2017053274 (print) | LCCN 2017055354 (ebook) | ISBN 9780802496386 | ISBN 9780802418074
Subjects: LCSH: Christianity and culture--United States. | Christianity—United States. | David, King of Israel. | Courage—Religious aspects—Christianity.
Classification: LCC BR526 (ebook) | LCC BR526 .M37 2018 (print) | DDC 241/.4--dc23
LC record available at https://lccn.loc.gov/2017053274

We hope you enjoy this book from Moody Publishers. Our goal is to provide high-quality, thought-provoking books and products that connect truth to your real needs and challenges. For more information on other books and products written and produced from a biblical perspective, go to www.moodypublishers.com or write to:

Moody Publishers
820 N. LaSalle Boulevard
Chicago, IL 60610

1 3 5 7 9 10 8 6 4 2

Printed in the United States of America

I dedicate this book to my fair Alice,
partner and best friend for nigh on forty years
as well as sainted mother of five, author,
beloved teacher, theologian extraordinaire, and
my personal guide always on the way to brave.

CONTENTS

FOREWORD

Knowing the past gives us courage to live in the present and to face the future bravely. Time and time again as I meandered slowly through *The Way to Brave*, this thought kept coming back to me: knowing the past empowers us to be courageous in the present. Moses knew this, David knew this, Jesus knew this, the apostles knew this.

Psalm 77 is my favorite passage in the Bible about going back to find courage for the present and future. This psalm of Asaph opens up in cries for help and sinks into helpless despair. Even the thought of God leads the psalmist to groan and faint. Too troubled to speak, fearing that God may have utterly rejected him and wondering if all his good days with God are behind him, he then turns to the past, to "the years when the Most High stretched out his right hand" (v. 10). His shift in tone from despair to courage occurs when he says "I will remember the deeds of the LORD" (v. 11). Then he ponders one mighty act of God after another, and by the time the psalmist finishes we simply start adding our own memories of what God has done in the past in our lives.

We need to turn our eyes, like the psalmist, from the worries of our world and the threats of our culture toward the covenant God made with us in Christ, toward the God who made that covenant, and toward the absolute faithfulness and reliability of that God.

Only in turning to God can we become brave enough to live today and face tomorrow. Only in watching the despairs of Good Friday turn into the triumphs of Easter will we find the way to brave.

Jesus embodied this kind of bravery: because He knew the God of Abraham and Moses was the great "I AM WHO I AM," because He knew the God who exiled the southern tribes to Babylon was the same God who made the path straight back to Jerusalem and because their redeeming God gave them courage to rebuild the city of Jerusalem when their enemies surrounded them. This is why Jesus told the disciples that He would both be crucified *and be raised again*. He bravely set His face toward Jerusalem because He knew what God had done in the past and therefore, with His trust in His Father as the God who turns exile into homecoming, God opened the tomb on Easter morning, and Jesus roamed the land once again. Think, too, of Paul. He was grieved over his people's rejection of the Messiah and three chapters in Romans (9–11) focus on his own turning to the past to face the future bravely. Knowing God's past mercy with Israel empowered him to know God's future mercy with Israel. He knows Israel's future because he knows the God of Israel's past.

McQuitty's focus on David turns us toward one of the great themes in the Bible: the God of the past reveals who God is, and that revelation empowers us to become courageous about the present and future, because our God is faithful to who He is. That God—the One who called Moses out of Egypt, the southern tribes back from Babylon, and Jesus to rise from the grave—is the God who calls us, who anoints us to bravery in the face of our Goliaths, to breaking us and testing us so He can train us in the way of faith. He is the same today as He was yesterday. That God, the God of our past, is the God of our present and our future. Our God is reliable and powerful.

There's a little bit for everyone in *The Way to Brave* as Pastor Andy McQuitty takes us into dimensions of the culture war and escapades in church history and gospel ministries that span the breadth of the church today. We will all find courage for today and hope for tomorrow in this noble exposition of David.

Scot McKnight
Julius R. Mantey Professor of New Testament
Northern Seminary
Lisle, Illinois

Prologue:

AN ANCIENT PROFILE IN COURAGE

The following is a partial retelling of 1 Samuel 17
(with some artistic liberty), which is the remarkable
true story of a shepherd lad's courage in challenging
a terrifying Philistine giant.

Even though it's been nearly three thousand years since David fought Goliath, the story of this teenaged Jewish shepherd stepping solo into an arena-like valley for single combat to the death with the celebrated warrior-giant of the Philistines is still as electrifying as the day it happened. For now, never mind the outcome of their confrontation. Just David's very willingness to lay his life on the line has got to be one of the greatest displays of unadulterated bravery ever seen on the face of this earth, and it forever enshrines his story as one of the world's greatest profiles in courage.

The encounter occurred on a lovely Judean spring morning in Israel's Valley of Elah just west of what soon would become the city of Jerusalem. Two mismatched armies were drawn up for battle. The well-armed Philistines' army encamped on the valley's southern slope. On the northern slope, Israel's soldiers were largely composed of a dismally armed band of dirt and sheep farmers. Due to a Philistine monopoly on metalworking, King Saul and his son

Jonathan were probably the only Israelite soldiers who wielded real swords that day. Yet, this ragtag band had miraculously thrashed the Philistines in a humiliating battle at Michmash just months earlier. Now the angry pagans wanted payback on those Jewish rogues, *big-time payback,* as in no-more-nation-of-Israel-after-this-goes-down payback.

No way **could a kid be that brave when all Israel's mighty warriors were so paralyzed by fear.**

The Israelites were understandably anxious as, for the fortieth day in a row, they warily watched their pagan enemies. The older soldiers spit and swore while the young bucks masked their fear with nervous jokes and braggadocio. That's how they waited for "it" to happen for the eightieth time that month, the second time that very day. Then, like clockwork, "it" did.

Moving with great fanfare down from the Philistine ranks was the Philistine champion, a singularly menacing incredible hulk and the Hebrews' worst nightmare. Goliath was the biggest and maddest and baddest nine-foot-nine-inch creature the Israelites had ever seen. Decked out in his 125-pound bronze suit of snake-scale armor, he sported a spear with a tip that weighed seventeen pounds and a caddy who carried, not golf clubs, but a shield big enough to shade a picnic or squash a platoon like a swarm of inebriated flies. (Let it be noted, the Israelite soldiers had no illusions that Goliath had come to provide shade for a picnic.)

Goliath wasted no time in turning the Israelites' battlefield butterflies into stark terror as he swaggered up to his usual taunting-spot with armor-bearer in tow. "Goliath stood and shouted to the ranks of Israel, 'Why do you come out and line up for battle? Am I not a Philistine, and are you not the servants of Saul? Choose a man and have him come down to me. If he is able to fight and kill me, we will become your subjects; but if I overcome him and kill him, you will become our subjects and serve us.' Then the Philistine said, 'This day I defy the armies of Israel! Give me a man and let us fight each other'" (1 Sam. 17:8–10). Obviously, there was a lot riding on that particular wager.

In modern PWA (Professional Wrestling Association) parlance, Goliath's pre-bout bellow amounted to the following challenge: "I dare you Israelite dingbats to come up with *a big enough fool* to fight me one-on-one, single combat, winner take all. I float like a butterfly and sting like a bee, but that's just the *hors d'oeuvres*. The main course is me crushing like a tank, and I have a strong hankering to serve that up to some unfortunate and foolish Hebrew right now." Goliath's mixed-metaphor speech had its desired effect. "On hearing the Philistine's words, Saul and all the Israelites were dismayed and terrified" (1 Sam. 17:11).

At that, the Israelite army prepared to do the only reasonable thing under the circumstances—turn tail and hoof it home for the eightieth time. Once again, the giant had rattled their cage. Once again, their hearts melted within them. Once again fear had seized them. So once again, they would lie down half-ashamed to sleep on Goliath's offer and pray for a better deal. Truth be told, hope was sorely waning that one would ever come.

But wait, right then it did . . . in the form of a 16-ish-year-old acne-faced shepherd kid named David, who had been pulled away from sheep duty and on to quartermaster duty for his dad, Jesse. Just that morning, he'd set out walking the fifteen miles from Bethlehem to deliver corned-beef-on-rye (actually, parched corn, bread, and cheese) to his older brothers, who were soldiers in King Saul's army. He arrived at Elah just in time to get both barrels of

Goliath's latest harangue and subsequently see his brothers cowering in fear with the rest of the army.

But David couldn't abide seeing the men of Israel cravenly folding under this pagan's verbal onslaught. He immediately found King Saul and volunteered to be Goliath's "big enough fool" to fight the Philistine Hulkster in single combat, winner take all, as Israel's champion. "David said to Saul, 'Let no one lose heart on account of this Philistine; your servant will go and fight him'" (v. 32).

What? Saul did a double take and then, flustered, replied: "You are not able to go out against this Philistine and fight him; you are only a young man, and he has been a warrior from his youth" (v. 33).

King Saul just could not believe the kid was this courageous. Surely David didn't grasp the seriousness of the situation. Didn't he realize (like everybody else) that he really wasn't volunteering to fight Goliath, but to die, fast, in a gory, gruesome fashion? Saul was incredulous in the face of David's offer to fight because in *no way* could a kid be that brave when all Israel's mighty warriors were so paralyzed by fear.

Even the reckless Saul did not savor seeing a shepherd-boy-massacre on his watch. And, upon finding out about their pipsqueak brother's brash offer to fight Goliath, neither did David's older brothers. They assumed he was grandstanding for the crowd because, as scared as they were of the giant, there's no way their little brother, the runt of Jesse's litter, *wasn't*. So David's brothers and King Saul's visceral response (as transliterated by the author) to David's desire to fight Goliath was straightforward: "No, Grasshopper, appreciate the offer, but you need to get a grip and ditch these grandiose notions of giant-slaying. Stop acting so high and mighty, deliver your deli, and run along home to your toy soldiers and filthy sheep." David, however, was calmly unmoved.

But David said to Saul, "Your servant has been keeping his father's sheep. When a lion or a bear came and carried off a sheep from the flock, I went after it, struck it and rescued the sheep from its mouth. . . . The LORD who rescued me from the paw of the lion and the paw of the bear will rescue me from the hand of this Philistine."

Saul said to David, "Go, and the LORD be with you." (vv. 34–35a, 37)

So David did. And so the Lord was. And so this story is . . . to be continued!

Introduction:

BEAUTIFUL AND TERRIBLE THINGS WILL HAPPEN

For it is you who light my lamp; the LORD my God lightens my darkness. For by you I can run against a troop, and by my God I can leap over a wall. This God— his way is perfect; the word of the LORD proves true; he is a shield for all those who take refuge in him. —DAVID, PSALM 18:28–30 ESV

I'm a great stickler for truth in advertising, so with hopes that you still have your return receipt if needed, let me make sure that the book you now hold in your hands is the book you actually think you hold in your hands. *The Way to Brave* is not a shortcut to courage or an instruction manual in bravado. It is not a self-management primer on how to stay cool under fire or a psychological study of self-coaching techniques to keep you calm in a crisis. Such books exist, and if that's what you're looking for, I encourage you to avoid feeling victimized by a "bait and switch" scheme and trade this title in for one of them. You'll be happier if you do, and believe me, so will I!

On the other hand, if you're taking a longer view and searching for a map of the path to a courageous soul, then *The Way to Brave* is just the book for you. It is God's biblical blueprint, not for action-film bravado or short bursts of ginned-up movie-star bravery, but for consistent courage, a sustained state of mind and heart, and intentional discipleship that goes the distance of years and not just minutes. There are no shortcuts to this kind of quiet, steady bravery in the hearts of God's children. It is the product of a Christian's determination to be "covered by the dust" (which I'll explain later) of their Master. Admittedly, the price of discipleship to be paid on this "way to brave" is steep, but the map is true and the results are supernatural. The way is costly, but the destination is glorious and the results nothing less than joyful.

Did you pick up on this from David's words in Psalm 18? "For it is you who light my lamp; the LORD my God lightens my darkness. For by you I can run against a troop, and by my God I can leap over a wall. This God—his way is perfect; the word of the LORD proves true; he is a shield for all those who take refuge in him" (Ps. 18:28–30 ESV). In the context of a world hostile to David's faith, those are the confident words of a humble young man, the joyful words of a trustful young man, and the grateful words of a blessed young man. But most of all, they are the *courageous* words of a *brave* young man that comply with Frederick Buechner's reassuring perspective: "Here is the world. Beautiful and terrible things will happen. Don't be afraid."[1]

David actually was not afraid in a world where beautiful and terrible things did indeed happen because he had a powerfully constructed faith of the lamp-lighting, darkness-illuminating, troop-running, wall-leaping, people-shielding, and giant-slaying variety. I seriously doubt that I'm alone in longing for that kind of faith in my own life, which, I suspect like yours, is increasingly being lived in this world of beautiful and terrible things. Don't you want to sign up for a "David faith," too?

Kansas No More

Dorothy once famously observed, "Toto, I've a feeling we're not in Kansas anymore." Due to the United States' unique founding on the principle of religious freedom, we Christians have for nearly three hundred years lived in our "Kansas"—a spiritual "Pax Americana" of sorts, during which the church enjoyed not only cultural acceptance, but the badge of spiritual entitlement as well. But no more. Long story short, the tables have turned. The American public square no longer honors fundamental Christian values. It rejects them. Sincere believers aren't emulated and admired. They're scapegoated and ridiculed by our culture's top four opinion-shaping institutions—government, media, the academy, and the entertainment industry.

A particularly egregious example of this "official" scorning of Christian values in the public square was Russ Vought's confirmation hearing in June 2017. As a nominee for deputy director of the Office of Management and Budget (OMB), he came before a US Senate Committee headed by Bernie Sanders for confirmation. The senator's hostile questioning of Vought had little to do with OMB but a whole lot to do with the theological excoriation of Christianity's core doctrine of salvation. The key exchange came at the end of Sanders's questioning:[2]

> **Sanders:** I understand you are a Christian, but this country is made of people who are not just—I understand that Christianity is the majority religion, but there are other

people of different religions in this country and around the world. In your judgment, do you think that people who are not Christians are going to be condemned?

Vought: Thank you for probing on that question. As a Christian, I believe that all individuals are made in the image of God and are worthy of dignity and respect regardless of their religious beliefs. I believe that as a Christian that's how I should treat all individuals.

Sanders: You think your statement that you put into that publication, they do not know God because they rejected Jesus Christ, His Son, and they stand condemned, do you think that's respectful of other religions?

Vought: Senator, I wrote a post based on being a Christian and attending a Christian school that has a statement of faith that speaks clearly in regard to the centrality of Jesus Christ in salvation.

Sanders: I would simply say, Mr. Chairman, that this nominee is really not someone who this country is supposed to be about.

That was a remarkable moment: a United States senator publicly rebuking a Christian nominee for public office on the grounds that his faith is not what "this country is supposed to be about." The statement was startling not only because Sanders's claim was outrageous and erroneous, but mainly because it was made so openly and explicitly. As such, it fit right in with other powerful voices in post-Christian America, like late-night cable "comedians" who regularly mock Christians on national TV, the major city mayor who sought to censor pastors' sermons,[3] civil liberties organizations that sue Christians' businesses dry,[4] and government agencies that indict Christian ministries and threaten

Christian universities[5] and churches.[6] Cheap shots and insinuations that Christianity "is really not something this country is supposed to be about" steadily gurgle up from the Oscars and the Grammys and from smarmy morning TV hosts and major city newspaper editors and celebrated university academics.

Here's the new reality about the American spiritual landscape going forward. We Christ followers will continue to find it harder and harder to catch a break in the very land of "in God we trust." Kansas? No, Toto, I'm reasonably sure we've been relocated.

Suddenly, finding our new address in a post-Christian, secularized American public square—our own "Valley of Elah"—is a rude and anxiety-producing awakening for many believers today. The hearts of many have become as fearful as the Israelite spies who went with Caleb to check out the Promised Land of Canaan only to find "people . . . there . . . of great size. We saw the Nephilim there (the descendants of Anak come from the Nephilim). We seemed like grasshoppers in our own eyes, and we looked the same to them'" (Num. 13:30–33). It's disconcerting to look next door and find our modern-day government, education, entertainment, and media Nephilim making us feel like grasshoppers by bellowing their steady playlist of mockery and marginalization of biblical values. It's undeniable. The ancient giant's taunts are once again being heard in the land of the free and the home of the brave.

Of Courage and Love

But dear friends, let not your hearts be troubled. *Take courage!*

Perhaps you read those two words and agree with Peter Mommsen:

At such a moment, being told to "take courage" can sound like a grim joke. No doubt that's how it sounded to the friends of Jesus who accompanied him on his last journey to Jerusalem, where he would be killed. Yet, as John reports in the sixteenth chapter of his Gospel, "Take courage!" was one of the last things Jesus told his disciples, just hours before his arrest and execution. He added, in a statement that must have puzzled them: "I have overcome the world."[7]

Sure, living a socially entitled faith in any country is always a more pleasant experience overall. But history proves that consistently pleasant experiences for the church over time have a debilitating effect on faith. Spiritual muscles atrophy, conviction softens, and courage wanes in an amicable environment where devotion to Christ is rarely (if ever) challenged. On the other hand, an increasingly hostile environment that challenges our devotion to Christ on a regular basis tones our spiritual muscles, drives conviction deep, and creates a great thirst for courage by reminding us of the fundamental reality of our life's journey. We are pilgrims and sojourners on a desperate quest from time to eternity with and to the One who first created and loved and redeemed us so that we might ultimately love Him back forever. It is good that our path be a desperate quest and not merely a pleasant jaunt, lest our faith become flabby and our character as faithful disciples of Christ be diminished in the shallows of safety. Our Lord has overcome the world, and He invites us to bask in His victory.

My main concern in these days is not that American Christians suddenly need courage in a big way, but rather that we pursue courage in the right way, and for the right reason. As God's beloved ones, we should celebrate "leaving Kansas" for propelling us to love our heavenly Father (the right reason) as fully formed, courageous disciples (the right way). As the apostle John insists, it is love for God that births true courage. "There is no fear in love. But perfect love drives out fear, because fear has to do with punishment. The one who fears is not made perfect in love" (1 John 4:18). The word "courage" itself is derived from the Latin "cor" (or "coer" from the later Anglo-French), which means "heart." No heart, no love. No love, no courage. No courage, no overcoming the world. But if there is heart and love, there will be courage, which the great St. Augustine saw simply

History proves that consistently pleasant experiences for the church over time have a debilitating effect on faith. Spiritual muscles atrophy, conviction softens, and courage wanes in an amicable environment where devotion to Christ is rarely (if ever) challenged.

as a form of "love ready to bear all things for God's sake."[8]

A David Faith in a Goliath World

As you and I seek courage to face a gathering spiritual storm in America, the new land of giants, we must begin by answering fundamental questions. Is love for God our ultimate motivation? And is our love for God sufficient to motivate us to do whatever it takes, to learn whatever we need to know, to live in whatever way necessary as followers of Christ to draw close to our heavenly Father and bring Him glory?

It was for David. His extraordinary courage in Elah was not a momentary surge of valor ignited by a few intense seconds of confrontation, but a consistent expression of faith forged through long years of discipleship. Many have wondered why, after God decided to end Saul's disobedient reign (1 Sam. 15), He took so long, up to ten years, to replace him with David.[9] My answer is: that's how long it took God to *prepare* David. When David appeared that day in Elah, he'd already been for years on the path of discipleship as an enrollee in God's program of shaping courageous souls. Because David had faithfully, lovingly, and hopefully completed that "way to brave," he already possessed marvelous, love-empowered courage.

In 1 Samuel 16, this became obvious when Samuel asked Jesse to present his seven sons so that one could be selected king. The eldest, Eliab, was almost a Saul-clone—so tall, so handsome that Samuel immediately concluded he had his guy. "But the LORD said to Samuel, 'Do not consider his appearance or his height, for I have rejected him. The LORD does not look at the things people look at. People look at the outward appearance, but the LORD looks at the heart'" (1 Sam. 16:7). God was commanding Samuel to behold, not His physical handiwork in Eliab's good looks, but His discipleship handiwork in David's faithful heart: "My heart, O God, is steadfast, my heart is steadfast" (Ps. 57:7). And so it was for David, not fickle and afraid but grateful and courageous, with eyes fixed on God long before his eyes fell on Goliath. David's words in Psalm 18 teach us that his courage in the Valley of Elah did not derive from fear overcome, but love pursued. "I *love* you, LORD, my strength. The LORD is my

> **David's extraordinary courage in Elah was not a momentary surge of valor ignited by a few intense seconds of confrontation, but a consistent expression of faith forged through long years of discipleship.**

rock, my fortress and my deliverer; my God is my rock, in whom I take refuge, my shield and the horn of my salvation, my stronghold. I called to the LORD, who is worthy of praise, and I have been saved from my enemies" (Ps. 18:1–3). David did not fight because God took away his fear. David fought because love empowered his faith.

Christian Community and the Way to Brave

Here's the good news for all of you who, like me, know you need courage now more than ever before in your life. David proves that there is no need for Christians to cower in fear during spiritually chaotic times! We can all be courageous and of good cheer in the land of giants. So can our children and parents and friends in Christ. We just need to allow God to shape our faith in our new land of giants in the same way He shaped David's faith for his Goliath world. God transformed David into a missionary-disciple with a steadfast soul. And He will do this for us Christ followers too, in and through our communities of faith, as our churches get back to the New Testament cultivation of faithful discipleship. Courage is not a singular virtue that can be sought in isolation. Rather (as we will explore in chapter 10), it's a by-product of authentic community, a bonus benefit that we receive in the package deal of love-induced discipleship focused on bearing one another's burdens and, as the church, being *with* God *for* blessing the world around us.

As God carefully and comprehensively prepared David, He wants to carefully and comprehensively prepare us too. He wants to grant to us the five specific assets that He granted to David and indeed, to all great servant leaders and missionary disciples throughout both Old and New Testament history: *a specific sense of calling to a clear mission, a divine anointing with accompanying empowerment, a noble character marked by humility, a tested and proven faith,* and *remarkable skill that is the fruit of consistent practice.* In each of the five sections of this book, we will examine David's preparation in these five key areas that, taken together, arguably made him history's greatest profile in courage. As we do so, history assures us that we can anticipate a great gift coming our way. God's preparation in the way to brave will equip us with courage too—that great serendipity of a powerfully constructed faith of the lamp-lighting, darkness-illuminating, troop-running, wall-leaping, and yes, giant-slaying variety. Beautiful and terrible things *will* happen in our world. But never fear. This world has already been overcome, and those of us following hard after Jesus, the Great Overcomer, are invited to reap the spoils as God shapes in us a David faith for a Goliath world.

Section 1

GOD
CALLS US

1 SAMUEL 16:1

The LORD said to Samuel, "How long will you mourn for Saul, since I have rejected him as king over Israel? Fill your horn with oil and be on your way; I am sending you to Jesse of Bethlehem. I have chosen one of his sons to be king."

THOUGH DAVID'S FATHER JESSE and his seven brothers (starting with Abinadab and Shammah) were surprised and somewhat agitated by this news, I do not believe that the shepherd boy David was. That wily old prophet Samuel had come already to the family spread to anoint a new king for Israel. But instead of choosing from the proffered lineup of Jesse's sons, he flabbergasted the family by elevating the kid who still had a scraggly beard and a sorry job.

So Samuel and, I'm surmising, David, were privy to a key piece of inside information. God had already chosen David to be king, not on the basis of his impressive appearance, but his godly heart (1 Sam. 16:7). Perhaps then from a distant hilltop, David sat watching the pure theater of Samuel's kingly audition of his brothers in nervous anticipation of the summons he surely knew would come. When David arrived, Samuel executed God's directive: "Rise and anoint him; this is the one" (1 Sam. 16:12). Hence was David called as King and thereby fortified with a unique sense of purpose for his life. Cian Power describes that purpose which David would have known was central to his calling as king:

> The king's role as judge, and as the advocate of the helpless, is described enthusiastically in Psalm 72. There, it is clear that his struggle for justice (Hebrew *mispat*) ensures more than just lawfulness; it brings peace and fertility, habitability, to his land. The king's relationship with the god of Israel, YHWH is . . . extremely close. Psalm 89 contains a beautifully symmetrical picture of YHWH, the king in heaven, and David, the king on earth. Both figures are beyond comparison with other beings in their realms, and YHWH guarantees victory and honor to David and his descendants. Here David seems to be the tool YHWH uses to rule on earth, his deputy or viceroy.[1]

Some months later, the shepherd boy interloper at the Valley of Elah stood wrapped in his calling as king like a knight wrapped in blue-steel armor. David's calling as king, yet unknown to Saul and most of the soldiers that day, made his decision to face Goliath merely academic. Anointed king, David's task as God's viceroy on behalf of His people on earth was clear: struggle for justice and bring peace, fertility, and habitability to His land. Goliath stood in the way of that good struggle, so David's sense of calling to a clear mission gave him confidence that drove away fear. He experienced the power of purpose famously described by George Bernard Shaw:

> This is the true joy in life, the being used for a purpose recognized by yourself as a mighty one; the being a force of nature instead of a feverish, selfish little clod of ailments and grievances complaining that the world will not devote itself to making you happy. I am of the opinion that my life belongs to the whole community, and as long as I live it is my privilege to do for it whatever I can. I want to be thoroughly used up when I die, for the harder I work the more I live. I rejoice in life for its own sake. Life is no "brief candle" for me. It is a sort of splendid torch which I have got hold of for the moment, and I want to make it burn as brightly as possible before handing it on to future generations.[2]

David knew he was called to be king, and the resulting clarification of his mission gave him confidence that, even though he had to face Goliath, the Valley of Elah was where God wanted his "splendid torch" to be lit. Knowing he was doing the right thing made David courageous, and it will likewise make Christians courageous in our post-Christian culture because we know with certainty and clarity our call from God in these days.

Chapter 1

GARDENS, NOT WALLS

Lord, make me an instrument of Thy peace. Where there is hatred, let me sow love. Where there is injury, pardon, Where there is doubt, faith. Where there is despair, hope. Where there is darkness, light. Where there is sadness, joy. O Divine Master, grant that I may not so much seek to be consoled as to console, To be understood as to understand, To be loved as to love. For it is in giving that we receive. It is in pardoning that we are pardoned. It is in dying that we are born to eternal life. Amen. —St. Francis of Assisi

May God be gracious to us and bless us and make his face shine on us— so that your ways may be known on earth, your salvation among all nations.

—Psalm 67:1–2

What on earth is God's calling for His heaven-bound people? Are we Christians supposed to build walls or plant gardens? That is the million-dollar question for American believers who've absconded from Kansas to the land of giants. If David's clear sense of calling made him brave, and if David's courage in his land of giants derived from knowing with certainty what God had assigned him to do, then logic dictates that knowing with certainty God's assignment will make us courageous too. Christ's call to His church, therefore, is the same as God's historical call to His people throughout history. It is not to build defensive walls to keep people far from God *out*, but rather to plant beautiful gardens, places of shalom, to beckon people far from God *in*.

So again, what on earth is God's calling for His heaven-bound people? Great question! And to get the answer, we must first understand the context. God's calling comes not in a vacuum, but against the background of human history in our fallen world. The first step in embracing our courage-inducing calling from God is to understand the human predicament that He's called us to help fix.

The Vandalism of Shalom[1]

At the Bible's beginning, we learn how our world became broken by the entrance of sin into Paradise. God Himself had planted the garden of Eden and not only made it a home for Adam and Eve, but also a place where peace (*shalom*, used 250 times in the Old Testament) prevailed.

Shalom for our ancient human forebears meant not only the absence of meaningless wars and frivolous lawsuits, but also the presence of completeness, wholeness, health, tranquility, prosperity, fullness, rest, and harmony in their relationships with God, each other, themselves, and the whole creation.[2] Sounds like Adam and Eve had scored a trip to Fantasy Island (a TV series that debuted in 1977, for my younger readers who know only Jeff Probst's *Survivor* today!), right? But no. It was way better (they didn't need the diminutive Tattoo to announce their arrival by

> **Christ's call to His church, therefore, is the same as God's historical call to His people throughout history. It is not to build defensive walls to keep people far from God *out*, but rather to plant beautiful gardens, places of shalom, to beckon people far from God *in*.**

ringing a bell and yelling, "De plane, Boss, De Plane!" And besides, as cool as Ricardo Montalban was as Mr. Roarke, he wasn't divine). Far from a merely expensive, exotic vacation, God Himself had created people from the beginning to live forever in this breathtakingly beautiful, shalom-dripping garden as their home.

Therein lies the epic tragedy of Eden's destruction through the vandalism of shalom. We had it made in the shade (literally) but blew it all in a sinful power play with a huge generational price tag: Paradise Lost (with apologies to John Milton).

That first power play happened not in a hockey rink or on Wall Street or in a political smoke-filled room, but in a garden, in *the* garden . . . of Eden. You can read all about it in Genesis 3. The Enemy of God and humans, Satan, disguised as a snake, found a soft spot in Eve's and Adam's new human hearts. "God knows that when you eat the fruit, your eyes will be opened and you will be like God, knowing good and evil." Hmmm! Eve had just been invited to put the crown on and see how it felt to have *real* power and be empowered to get *whatever* she wanted at God's and others' expense. Adam also chimed in with the thought that he better look out for himself since he's the Number One man. So they essentially told God to take a hike and they'd look after their own affairs from now on.

This bone-headed decision (which you and I would probably have made as well!) was an expression of human pride and will for power ("be like God"), which the Lord obviously could not abide. Just as there's no way Fantasy Island could survive with people who had made its destruction their goal, Adam and Eve were ejected from Eden, estranged from God, and consigned to conflict within themselves, among themselves, and even with the created order. They (and all of us humans ever since) paid an egregious price for that forbidden bite, which the serpent failed to mention:

estrangement from their Father God and the jettisoning of their shalom . . . and ours too. "If only you had paid attention to my commands, your peace would have been like a river, your well-being like the waves of the sea" (Isa. 48:18). "If only," indeed! Augustine's famous opening to his *Confessions* acknowledges our loss: "you made us for yourself and our hearts find no peace until they rest in you."[3] The entrance of sin into Eden through the rebellion of our human forebears resulted in profound broken-ness for people and creation itself, shattering God's perfect peace and creating ugly places. As Dr. Barry Jones explains, "When sin enters the story, shalom is vandalized. God's glorious intention for his good creation is subverted. The wholeness and harmony we were created to enjoy with God, with each other, with creation and with ourselves is fundamentally violated."[4]

And the beat goes on. Shalom violated in Eden becomes shalom vandalized in history. Human pride's decision to compete with God by attempting to become like God explains why broth-ers and sisters feud and why marriages shatter and why neigh-bors fight and churches split and friendships end. It explains why alliances disintegrate and why treaties fail and why nations fight. War itself, you see, is a symptom of the fear-inducing van-dalism of shalom in a million individual human hearts! As the Associated Press reported, "For four decades a gut-level ingredi-ent of democracy—trust in the other fellow—has been quietly draining away. These days, only one-third of Americans say most people can be trusted. Half felt that way in 1972. . . . Forty years later, a record high of nearly two-thirds say 'you can't be too care-ful' in dealing with people."[5] In a similar vein, Ray Pritchard re-ports that "Psychology Today posed this intriguing question, 'If you could push a button and eliminate any person with no re-percussions to yourself, would you do it?' Sixty percent of those responding answered yes. One man posed an even better question, 'If such a device were invented, would anyone live to tell about it?'"[6] That simple question exquisitely frames the vandalism of shalom in our world.

The Shalom Restoration Project Begins

If vandalized shalom is the problem, then restored shalom is the solution. But can that happen, and if it does, what does it look like? In his 2008 novel *The Cellist of Sarajevo*, Steven Galloway offers us intriguing answers in fictionalizing the historical account of Vedran Smailović an opera cellist who became famous during the siege of Sarajevo in the Bosnian War. Each day, citizens struggled to find food and water while living in constant fear of bombshells, mortars, and sniper bullets. Smailović lived near one of the few working bakeries, where a line of twenty-two people had gathered on May 26, 1992. On that terrible morning, a mortar shell fell in their midst, killing all. Vedran rushed to the scene and melted in grief at the carnage he encountered. The next day, he returned to that very spot wearing black tails and tie. He sat with his cello on a fire-scorched chair in the bomb crater and performed Albioni's "Adagio in G Minor." His evocative playing drew a large crowd in spite of the danger of an attack, and when he was finished, there was a moment of profound silence followed by thunderous applause. "Oh thank you, this is what we so desperately needed!" shouted hundreds through broken voices and flowing tears.

For the next twenty-two days, one for each victim of the bombing, Smailović mitigated the ugliness of war with his only weapon—the beauty of his music. Sniper fire still sprayed around him, and mortars still rained down in the neighborhood, but he never stopped playing. His music created an oasis amidst the horror, an alternate vision of beauty that offered momentary respite to the people of Sarajevo as well as a challenge to those who were destroying the city. A "place-maker of peace," he became known as the "Cellist of Sarajevo," who offered the blessing of peace, if only locally and momentarily, to a shalom-vandalized city.

In so doing, Vedran merely participated in God's thousands-of-years-old shalom-restoration project that was launched in the very beginning pages of the Bible. God's plan called for the vandalism of shalom to be mitigated by blessing-bearing shalom place-makers.

> The LORD had said to Abram, "Go from your country, your people and your father's household to the land I will show you. I will make you into a great nation, and I will bless you; I will make your name great, and you will be a blessing. I will bless those who bless you, and whoever curses you I will curse; and all peoples on earth will be blessed through you." (Gen. 12:1–3)

Walter C. Kaiser Jr., summarizes the ultimate import of these verses (more commonly known as the Abrahamic covenant). "The message and its content, in fact the whole purpose of God, was that He would make a nation, give them a 'name,' bless them so that they might be light to the nations and thereby be a blessing to all the nations. To shrink back would be evil on Israel's part. Israel was to be God's missionary to the world—and so are we [church] by the same verses. The mission has not changed in our own day."[7] Vedran Smailović proves that last point. In becoming the "Cellist of Sarajevo," he just fell in line with God's ancient program for His people as played out on the pages of Scripture.

Pockets of Peace

I am so glad that Abram obeyed God's invitation to leave his comfy pad in Ur of the Chaldees to restore shalom in a broken world by being God's blessing-bearer. He stepped out in faith, and God honored him by changing his name to "Father of Nations." History shows that his descendants, the Israelites, would carry on God's shalom-restoration project as place-makers of peace. For example, when God raised up Moses to set the people free from slavery in Egypt and lead them home in the Exodus, the first oasis Israel reached in the wilderness was "Bethelim" (Hebrew for "house of palms"). At "Elim," twelve springs fed seventy palm trees. This was a beautiful metaphor for the covenant mission of the twelve Hebrew tribes among the seventy nations of the world at that time. Elim was a little Eden, a place of shalom and refreshment in the wilderness, a foretaste of the Promised Land, and a place of peace in the wilderness. Already the descendants of Abraham were getting their groove back as the "Cellists of Sand City"!

Moving along to the seventh century BC, we find the prophet Jeremiah with the unenviable job of writing to some ten thousand Jewish captives who had been taken in the first exile to Babylon when Nebuchadnezzar initially defeated King Jehoiachin in 605 BC. No wonder he bore the moniker "Weeping Prophet." His task was to encourage the captives to make the best of a very unhappy situation, because they were going to be stuck in it for seventy years! So how did he do it? By assuring them of God's future comfort? No. He reminded them of God's ancient calling in this letter sent from Jerusalem:

This is what the Lord Almighty, the God of Israel, says to all those I carried into exile from Jerusalem to Babylon: "Build

houses and settle down; plant gardens and eat what they produce. Marry and have sons and daughters; find wives for your
sons and give your daughters in marriage, so that they too
may have sons and daughters. Increase in number there; do
not decrease. Also, seek the peace and prosperity of the city
to which I have carried you into exile. Pray to the LORD for it,
because if it prospers, you too will prosper." (Jer. 29:4–7)

I daresay this was not the first message the Israelites in
Babylon wanted to hear! Organize as rebels into little platoons of
military resistance? Ah, that might have been more satisfying. Or
at least wall yourselves off into righteous little silos where those
big bad Babylonian bullies can't sully your tender conscience with
their persistent badgering! That might have been more reassuring. But no. Through the prophet, God was calling His blessed
people to bless their captors, even though they were literally foreigners and exiles. He instructed them to "seek the peace and
prosperity of the city" by becoming active cultural agents, even
in sin-broken Babylon. This meant carving out beautiful pockets
and places and expressions of shalom in the midst of very painful
pockets and places and expressions of ugliness in the capital city
of their enemy.

Here is the irony. Many of the exiles God was calling to
become place-makers of peace in Babylon had been perpetrators
of injustice in Judah. Earlier the prophet Jeremiah had channeled
God's heart on the matter: "This is what the LORD says: Do what
is just and right. Rescue from the hand of the oppressor the one
who has been robbed. Do no wrong or violence to the foreigner,
the fatherless or the widow, and do not shed innocent blood in
this place. For . . . if you do not obey these commands, declares
the LORD, I swear by myself that this palace will become a ruin'"

(Jer. 22:3–5). Sure enough, they didn't, and it did, and so we observe that the Lord feels strongly about injustice anytime, anywhere. "For I, the LORD, love justice; I *hate* robbery and wrongdoing" (Isa. 61:8).

It's safe to conclude that God hates the sin of injustice for the simple reason that it's just more vandalism of shalom. He hates the powerful and rich oppressing the powerless and poor through dishonor, robbery, and physical violence because it's just more breaking of peace. He hates injustice whether it shows up as cronyism, racism, classism, sexism, or fascism. He hates it whether it works its way out through back-scratching, power plays, unholy alliances, or unbridled lusts. Neal Plantinga cogently explains why: "God hates sin not just because it violates his law but because it violates shalom, because it breaks the peace, because it interferes with the way things are supposed to be . . . we may safely describe evil as any spoiling of shalom, whether physically (e.g., by disease), morally, spiritually, or otherwise."[8]

In Babylon, God wanted His people to learn new ways by remembering an old way. No longer were they to vandalize shalom. Instead, they would create safe havens for shalom. No longer would God's people act out a nightmare of injustice. Instead, they would live out God's dream of a world set right and thereby restore desperately needed pockets and places of shalom in a chaotic world.

> Is not this the kind of fasting I have chosen: to loose the chains of injustice and untie the cords of the yoke, to set the oppressed free and break every yoke? Is it not to share your food with the hungry and to provide the poor wanderer with shelter—when you see the naked, to clothe them, and not to turn away from your own flesh and blood? Then your light

will break forth like the dawn, and your healing will quickly appear; then your righteousness will go before you, and the glory of the LORD will be your rear guard. (Isa. 58:6–8)

In other words, God wants our first impulse in reversing injustice's vandalism of shalom to be garden-planting, not wall-building. Surely there will be times (as there have always been) when the people of God must stand their ground and build strong walls of truth and protection. But may our hearts' main inclination be to planting all the gardens we possibly can.

Jesus' Dream of a World Set Right

This Old Testament dream of a world set right was the object of Jesus' own earthly mission.

He went to Nazareth, where he had been brought up, and on the Sabbath day he went into the synagogue, as was his custom. He stood up to read, and the scroll of the prophet Isaiah was handed to him. Unrolling it, he found the place where it is written: "The Spirit of the Lord is on me, because he has anointed me to proclaim good news to the poor. He has sent me to proclaim freedom for the prisoners and recovery of sight for the blind, to set the oppressed free, to proclaim the year of the Lord's favor." Then he rolled up the scroll, gave it back to the attendant and sat down. The eyes of everyone in the synagogue were fastened on him. He began by saying to them, "Today this scripture is fulfilled in your hearing." (Luke 4:16–21)

Jesus' amazing self-introduction through the reading of the Isaiah scroll blew the socks (or if you will, sandals) off His

Nazarene listeners in the synagogue that day. He directly claimed to be the heaven-sent King who had come to bring justice and restore shalom! It was the great apostle Paul who later explained that Christ inaugurated the church's role in God's great shalom-restoration project by dying on Calvary's cross in our stead. "Therefore, since we have been justified through faith, we have peace with God through our Lord Jesus Christ, through whom we have gained access by faith into this grace in which we now stand" (Rom. 5:1–2). Shalom is essentially the Old Testament word for salvation. It means to be rightly related to God and others, so that God's gifts flow freely to you and through you. Clement of Alexandria put it this way in his translation of Matthew 5:9: "Blessed are those who have stilled the incredible battle which goes on in their own souls." That's exactly what happens when we are reconciled to God through Jesus Christ. Hearts are no longer troubled but blanketed by peace because the very harmony God had given Adam and Eve in the garden is restored.

Jesus, then, is the King who died to rescue God's people from the vandalism of shalom and to restore them to the beauty of shalom. No wonder Isaiah calls Him "Prince of Peace [*sar shalom*]" (9:6). Shalom was a big deal for Jesus. So it should not surprise us that a main goal of the prayer He taught us to pray was to lead the church to be not only the world's primary *beneficiaries* of shalom but also the world's primary *place-makers* of it: "This, then, is how you should pray: 'Our Father in heaven, hallowed be your name, your kingdom come, your will be done, on earth as it is in heaven'" (Matt. 6:9–10). If that prayer were answered, if the kingdom of God, whose Prince is "Sar Shalom," showed up in the day-to-day realities of our life and world, it would look like a community of people pursuing shalom by seeing, feeling, and responding with the heart of God to brokenness and injustice in the world.

Jesus was always engaging people— even people who didn't necessarily want to be engaged, like the woman who sneaked up to touch His robe or the tax- collector who was hiding in the tree.

We know this because that's precisely what the kingdom looked like during Jesus' earthly ministry, in which He powerfully modeled shalom place-making and seed-planting for us. Jesus was always taking careful note of people, recognizing not only their deep need but also their inner beauty: a widow on her way to the cemetery to bury her only son, a blind man by the side of the road, a man in the crowd with a withered hand, children who were eager to be blessed. He was always engaging people—even people who didn't necessarily want to be engaged, like the woman who sneaked up to touch His robe or the tax-collector who was hiding in the tree. Jesus reached out to them and engaged them in conversation, not to embarrass them, but to let them know they mattered, to plant the seeds of shalom. He did this in such a way that they were spurred on to follow Him, to renounce their sins, to turn from their self-focused lives. As He planted seeds, He cultivated growth in people in unexpected ways.

Jesus "planted gardens" at a sorrowful Samaritan well, a despairing Jerusalem pool, a skeptical fisherman's boat, the struggling-to-believe side of a mountain, the glory-infused top of a mountain, a self-righteous Pharisee's house, a forgiven tax-collector's party, the imposing Temple Courts, a garden of agony (Gethsemane), a high priest's great room turned courtroom, a Roman arena of scourging, and the shore of a storm-tossed sea. People flocked to Jesus' places of peace and there found the incredible blessings of transformation, faith, and restoration to shalom.

Gardens, Not Walls

When I realized that Jesus was the ultimate fulfillment of the Abrahamic covenant, I had my answer to this chapter's opening question: What on earth is God's calling for His heaven-bound people? Are we supposed to build walls or plant gardens? I now knew that getting a spiritual green thumb was my calling!

This was a revelation to me. For many years of my ministry as a pastor, I'd thought wall-building was my assigned task. After all, God calls us Christians to holiness, right? So surely walls must be built to keep the evil out. God calls us Christians to righteousness, right? So surely walls must be built to keep the troops in (line). God calls us to justice, right? So surely walls must be built to threaten injustice, right? Surely. But really? I was never quite sure, and that uncertainty kept me restless through the "culture wars" of the last generation. One example of how all of that came together for me occurred all the way back in 1991. As the senior pastor of Irving Bible Church (IBC), I joined Operation Rescue and started getting myself thrown in the hoosegow for illegally (though passively) blocking the Routh Street (Dallas) Abortion Clinic's doors during their peak business hours on Saturday. I'd go down to that infamous abortuary on Saturdays with a group of my culture-warrior friends (once with the newly converted Norma McCorvey, the original "Jane Roe" of the infamous 1973 Supreme Court case) with my game-face on and my Bible verses proving the humanity of unborn children at the ready. I did not appreciate the "pain grips" that the Dallas police dutifully but unnecessarily applied to our necks to keep this passive, frumpy group of Ghandi-like protesters under control as they hauled us away to the paddy wagons. But I confess I did truly understand their aggravation at (I'm sure) an inordinate number of sore "Blue" backs due to our impertinent insistence that the police carry us like so many sacks of uncooperative potatoes. (I confess that I enjoyed that part. A lot.) And I also must confess that, on the occasion of my first incarceration, I enjoyed the shocked look on then Dallas Seminary President Dr. Donald K. Campbell's face when I was unexpectedly able to introduce him as the preacher at IBC that Sunday because I was released earlier than expected from Dallas's Lew Sterrett Correctional Facility. He didn't know what I'd been up to until I said, "So glad I could get out of jail in time to introduce you, Dr. Campbell." His face turned three shades of red as he replied, "Um, thanks very much, I think." Hey, my newly created rap sheet was just an emblem of my contribution to the culture war, the latest volley in fulfilling my perceived purpose of fighting the good fight by building a big wall.

All that changed when it became clear to me that God wanted me to plant gardens, not build walls, and that getting a spiritual green thumb and not notches on my spiritual pistol-grip was my calling. God doesn't always call His people to be spiritual Seal Team Six fighters, but many times He calls us to be shalom-restoring ambassadors and place-makers of peace: "All this is from God, who reconciled us to himself through Christ and gave us the ministry of reconciliation: that God was reconciling the world to himself in Christ, not counting people's sins against them. And he has committed to us the message of reconciliation. We are therefore Christ's ambassadors, as though God were making his appeal through us. We implore you on Christ's behalf: Be reconciled to God" (2 Cor. 5:18–20).

Jesus is the Master Gardener. He desires that people far from God would find shalom in the gardens He has planted. He is calling people far from God into the garden. As Simon Holt expresses it, "Far from the task of rescuing people from the world, the mission of the church is to embody the transformative presence of God in and for it."[9] There it is again. Do you see it? "Blessed to be a blessing." N. T. Wright says it a different way. "We are called to be part of God's new creation, called to be agents of that new creation here and now. We are called to model and display that new creation in symphonies and family life, in restorative justice and poetry, in holiness and service to the poor, in politics and painting."[10] Whoa now! Could the good Dr. Wright say again what our calling is, please? "Called to be agents of [the] new creation." I believe another way of saying it is that we are called to be place-makers of peace, shalom restoration artists, or the "Cellists of the Cosmos" (with apologies to Vedran Smailović!) if you will.

Beautiful Purpose, Amazing Courage

It's a most beautiful calling, don't you think? And fundamentally simple, too, as defined by Andy Crouch: "Likewise our mission is not primarily to 'engage the culture' but to 'love our neighbor.' Our neighbor is not an abstract collective noun, but a real person in a real place . . . we will be ready to be the people of God in our cities and neighborhood, among every ethnicity and nation, living faithfully within our particular cultures and trusting God to weave out of our faithfulness the cosmic redemption he has promised and accomplished through his Son. Which is to say, we will be 'the church.'"[11] That's the kind of church we at Irving Bible Church are striving to become these days—a gathering of ambassadors of reconciliation and place-makers of shalom and the "Cellists of Dallas/Ft. Worth." Our commitment has emboldened us to take "A Transformed People, A Transformed City" as our immediate goal. It has also fortified our resolve to fulfill our "unofficially official" church motto in sometimes crazy, risky ways.

"We want to be such a blessing to our neighbors that, if money problems ever made us shut our doors, people in our parish would raise the funds to keep us in business."

That's precisely what IBCer Jessie Yearwood did in the weeks following the July 7, 2016, shooting tragedy in which five Dallas police officers were killed and nine injured while, ironically, protecting thousands who were protesting police that day. The horrific tragedy began on Dallas's Main Street and ended at El Centro College, where Jessie has been a longtime teacher and president of the faculty association. In the days that followed, she was one of the few people allowed on campus while the FBI conducted its investigation. That's when, sensing great need, Jessie responded as a place-maker of peace. As the campus reopened to staff, Jessie organized a team of faculty to create a special "shalom" experience. Local restaurants had brought so much food to feed the investigators that Jessie's team was able to take the leftovers and set up long tables designed to help their colleagues "lighten the load over a meal." "No one was allowed to come pick up food and leave," she says, "everyone had to stay and talk and connect." Jessie called the tables "healing tables," and they lived up to their name as the hospitality and conversations people experienced there jump-started the entire healing process at El Centro. Now a year later, Jessie explains her "Cellist of Sarajevo" heart as someone God used to bring shalom to hurting people. "On campus, I'm a secret agent, so to speak. Teaching is a cover for the relationships that I build. Those people eventually move on and build their lives, and that's okay. The Lord just intersects where He needs to." Here's how IBC's Pastor of Communications, Scott McClellan, who interviewed Jessie for this story, concluded his blog: "At the end of our conversation, I asked Jessie if she'd be open to me sharing her story with the people of IBC. She paused for a moment, then agreed on one condition: 'If it helps the body understand that we don't have to be special in terms of how God shows up when we don't expect him to. And if it helps people see how the mission of God shows up in these unusual ways.' . . . We can't control when or where tragedy will strike in a broken world, but we can set tables of healing amid the wreckage and watch God work."[12]

Indeed we can set tables. Indeed we must. Our calling as God's people is to be place-makers of peace, cellists of Sarajevo, setters of tables of healing amid the wreckage of our broken world. The good news about this for me is that my newly realized calling, as far as I can see, is a game changer, because it omits any immediate trips back to jail and keeps me intrepid in the meantime. I hope it will be so for you as well! May the beauty and specificity of God's calling to plant gardens (instead of building walls) generate courage in your soul, because to make places of peace in the sometimes chaotic, ugly, and even dangerous places in our lives and world requires us to be not only energetic, but brave. So my friends, let's hoist our cellos into the bomb crater and play our hearts out for the beat-down people gathered there, for blessed are those who fulfill God's call to be blessings as place-makers of peace.

Shalom.

Chapter 2

SERVANT EXILES

Dear friends, I urge you, *as foreigners and exiles*, to abstain from sinful desires, which wage war against your soul. Live such good lives among the pagans that, though they accuse you of doing wrong, they may see your good deeds and glorify God on the day he visits us. —1 Peter 2:11–12

But you, man of God, flee from all this, and pursue righteousness, godliness, faith, love, endurance and gentleness. Fight the good fight of the faith. . . . Timothy, guard what has been entrusted to your care. Turn away from godless chatter and the opposing ideas of what is falsely called knowledge, which some have professed and in so doing have departed from the faith.
—1 Timothy 6:11–12, 20–21

I was greatly encouraged and not just a little bit relieved to finally realize that my calling as a Christian in post-Christian America was not to build walls, but to plant gardens. This meant I could be the "Cellist of Sarajevo" instead of being the trustee delivering bologna sandwiches to the inmates during my intermittent stints at Lew Sterrett Jail. Thank God He calls His people to be place-makers of peace and blessed-to-be-a-blessing shalom-restorers. That's the "what" (we're supposed to do). But there's also a "how" (we're supposed to do it). God calls us in His church to be blessing-bearers and garden-planters with a very specific posture vis-à-vis our culture. We are not called to fight culture wars, but we must engage in spiritual warfare as peaceable warriors, fighting the good fight of faith and truth with both firm conviction and servant-hearted blessing. As Peter writes, "Dear friends, I urge you, *as foreigners and exiles*, to abstain from sinful desires, which *wage war* against your soul. Live such good lives among the pagans that, though they accuse you of doing wrong, they may see your good deeds and glorify God on the day he visits us" (1 Peter 2:11–12).

That's exactly what David did when pursued into the wilderness of En Gedi by a King Saul (and three thousand men) made insanely jealous by David's glorious defeat of Goliath. David didn't capitulate to Saul's unjust persecution by just giving up. Instead, he took the posture of a peaceable warrior. Saul made the unfortunate choice to use a cave where David was hiding out as his afternoon "rest stop." David "crept up unnoticed and cut off a corner of Saul's robe" (1 Sam. 24:4) to demonstrate that he could have killed this tormentor who had falsely accused him. But instead, David chose to honor him as God's anointed and spoke these words: "See, my father, look at this piece of your robe in my hand! I cut off the corner of your robe but did not kill you. See that there is nothing in my hand to indicate that I am guilty of wrongdoing or rebellion" (v. 11). David thus models for us the strategy that Peter laid out for God's "foreigner and exiles" to "live such good lives among the pagans that, though they accuse you of doing wrong, they may see your good deeds and glorify God." Later, David attributed God's deliverance from Saul in that cave to a crystal-clear

We are not called to fight culture wars, but we must engage in spiritual warfare as peaceable warriors, fighting the good fight of faith and truth with both firm conviction and servant-hearted blessing.

conscience. "I have not turned away from his decrees. I have been blameless before him and have kept myself from sin. The LORD has rewarded me according to my righteousness, according to the cleanness of my hands in his sight" (Ps. 18:22–24). Those are the words of a powerfully powerless peaceful warrior.

The Powerfully Powerless

At first blush, God's instructions for dealing with people who "accuse [us] of doing wrong" seem counterintuitive. A normal array of Christian responses to a hostile culture would seem limited to isolation (hunkering down behind circled wagons), escalation (getting bellicose in a renewed culture war), or assimilation (capitulating through all-out surrender). But as we saw in the last chapter, God's calling is a better fourth option. "Live such good lives among the pagans that . . . they may see your good deeds and glorify God on the day he visits us" (1 Peter 2:12). Sounds an awful lot like "Seek the peace and prosperity of the city to which I have carried you into exile," does it not? So, Peter defines that fourth option in terms of posture. Our cultural attitude and perspective as Christians is to be not one of power and entitlement, but one of servanthood and humility. We are *not* called to subdue our pagan culture through the shrewd manipulation of political power and insider stratagems, but subversively win it over by living Christlike lives as foreigners and exiles.

"Foreigners" are Christians who resonate with Jim Reeves's classic lyrics: "This world is not my home, I'm just passing through, my treasures are laid up somewhere beyond the blue."[1] "Exiles" (*parapedemois*, also translated "sojourners," "pilgrims," and "strangers") are blood-bought believers whose ultimate commitment to honor Jesus with their obedience has made them *parapedemois* no matter where in this world they live. Dr. Richard John Neuhaus summarizes the resulting posture of foreigners and exiles: "Christians are a pilgrim people, a people on the way, exiles from our true home, aliens in a strange land. And yet this strange land is very much our land, even if only for the duration of our exile, which is likely to be long."[2]

During our newly imposed exile as foreigners in America, we Christians are just going to have to lose our nostalgia for the 1950s and '60's "Leave it to Beaver" church world and get excited about being who we truly are—increasingly powerless spiritual minorities in a pagan culture. As a "pilgrim people," our call as the church is to shalom place-making, not ruling; to a servant's presence of blessing in the world, not a warm welcome from the world. Contrary to much of the church's historical practice, Jesus does *not* send us as bearers of His gospel as powerful (as in, triumphant) ones, but powerless ones. He doesn't send us in His name like judges or sheriffs or politicians, but *servants!* That posture strikes the wise as an actual advantage and not a demotion because they understand it's the most influential posture of all. As Bryan Stone writes, "Ironically, it may be that it is precisely from a position of marginality that the church is best able to announce peace and to bear witness to God's peaceable reign in such a way as to invite others to take seriously the subversive implications of that reign. It may be that through humility, repentance, and disavowal of its former advantages, so that those things which once were 'gains' the church now comes to regard as 'loss' (Phil 3.7), a church at the periphery of the world may yet be a church for the world."[3]

Counterintuitive? Most certainly. But intuitively undeniable? Yes, that too! Take the 1998 movie *Simon Birch* as an example. Based on John Irving's novel *A Prayer for Owen Meany*, it is the story of twelve-year-old Simon Birch who, despite his physical handicaps, believes God has a great purpose for his life. Simon was born with an abnormally small heart and was expected to die within the first twenty-four hours of his life. He surprised everyone, though, by living to be an adolescent. A disappointment to his parents and the target of many childhood pranks because of his miniature size and odd-sounding voice, Simon still believes that God will use him in a heroic way and seeks that open door. But Joe, Simon's best friend, doesn't believe in open doors because he doesn't believe in God at all.

One day Simon is riding with his classmates in a school bus on an icy road. The bus driver veers to avoid a deer, and the bus plunges into an icy lake. Simon and other students in the back of the bus are trapped as the bus begins to sink. Simon takes charge. He opens a window and calmly directs his panicked classmates to climb out. Last of all, Simon escapes into the icy water, where his weak heart is fatally damaged. In the hospital following the incident, Joe assures Simon that all the kids are all right. Simon asks, "Did you see how the children listened to me because of the way I looked?" Seconds later, Simon dies, knowing that God used him. But what Simon doesn't know is that his unwavering faith and servant's heart, not in spite of but because of his physical powerlessness, would become legendarily influential. Some twenty years later, standing at Simon's gravestone, Joe (now grown up) says, "I am doomed to remember a boy with a wrecked voice, not because of his voice or because he was the smallest person I ever knew, or even because he was the instrument of my mother's death, but because he is the reason I believe in God. What faith I have, I owe to Simon Birch, the boy I grew up with in Gravedown, Maine."[4] Little body and squeaky voice, yes, but also a courageous kid with a servant's heart. Treated like a foreigner and exile because of his differences in a small Maine town, he exerted an eternal influence on people because they saw his good deeds and could not but glorify the God who made them possible. A powerless Christian kid at the periphery of the world had become a kid for the world, and everyone knew it, and many were changed by it. Now just take a whole bunch of Simon Birches and put them together, and you have the church. God calls us to do exactly the same thing in our church communities with the exact same powerless posture, which Simon shows is actually the most powerful posture of all.

Doorkeepers

The Old Testament offers us a helpful metaphor for the posture of a church at the periphery of the world: "I would rather be a doorkeeper in the house of my God than dwell in the tents of the wicked" (Ps. 84:10). Psalm 84 is "of the sons of Korah," who were Levitical keepers of the gates of the tabernacle and later (1 Chron. 9) to the temple—the dwelling place of God in the midst of His blessed-to-be-a-blessing people and forerunner of the church—the shalom-infused community of Christ followers. It was their job to open the doors every morning to help feed the beggars who had gathered outside God's house. Even when these poor sought help after dark, the doorkeepers showed the way with lanterns through the doors that they kept to the place of peace within.

God's doorkeepers were not armed guards or political operatives or moral policemen. Their posture was not one of power brokers, but of servants. Their calling was to open the doors of God's house as foreigners and exiles, inviting people into a place of peace that stood in stark contrast to the surrounding culture of oppression and hatred. Like Simon Birch, their influence was a function not of their power, but rather of their countercultural, faithful servanthood, which they so gratefully realized was having an amazing impact in the land of giants. "I would *rather* be a doorkeeper in the house of my God . . ."! No wonder. And what a privilege that God is calling us as the church to be a bunch of countercultural, Simon Birch doorkeepers in our land of giants. In *Good Faith*, David Kinnaman and Gabe Lyons say that being countercultural is "not about raising our voices to drown out dissenters or making laws to make everyone behave nicely . . . being countercultural means bringing good faith—a vision for what is orderly and right, abundant and generous, beautiful and flourishing with life and relationships—to the broader culture. This vision is not just an individual pursuit; it is best expressed in communities of faith where believers love and care for one another well and then invite others in to experience the same grace."[5]

Yes, you and I are foreigners and exiles in our land of giants. But that's fine by me because God also says we're doorkeepers for that wonderful place of peace called the church, the community of faith. As doorkeepers, we have been inside, but we also go outside. We love what's inside, but also go outside because we so want to help outside people get in! We doorkeepers aren't there to erect barriers, but to remove them. We're not about closing doors on people, but about throwing them open for people! As Christian doorkeepers in the house of God, our job is never to block the way, but to clear the way for people to come to God! Our message to oppressed and heartbroken people struggling to know

> **We're doorkeepers for that wonderful place of peace called the church, the community of faith. As doorkeepers, we have been inside, but we also go outside. We love what's inside, but also go outside because we so want to help outside people get in!**

God in the land of giants is not, "Now's an inconvenient time," but "let me get that door for you!" Like Richard Peace says, "Christian conversion is about saying yes to Jesus, who has become for me a living person, who loves me and is willing to forgive me at that deep spot where I most need forgiveness. I say yes to joining up with his community and his way of living. I say yes to my spiritual aspirations, moving them from the periphery of my life to the very center. The aim of holy conversation is to help people as they walk on the road to conversion."[6]

God's Doorkeepers in Ancient Rome

So how does this doorkeeper, "foreigner and exile," Simon Birch posture of powerlessness actually work in the land of giants? Pretty amazingly well, as the early Christians in Rome demonstrated under the brutal persecution of Emperor Nero in the mid-60s of the first century. He falsely blamed Christians for the Great Fire of Rome and then visited upon them an unbelievably gory reign of terror. Even the Roman historian Tacitus (who was no Christian partisan) seems stunned by Nero's brutality when he wrote, "Besides being put to death [Christians] were made to serve as objects of amusement; they were clad in the hides of beasts and torn to death by dogs; others were crucified, others set on fire to serve to illuminate the night when daylight failed."[7]

Yet, these courageous Christ followers, though considered mere "objects of amusement" by Roman authorities, willingly suffered grief in these trials as servant exiles. They determined over the years to come that, at great cost to themselves, they would exercise God's fourth option in a decidedly hostile and chaotic place: "Seek the peace and prosperity of the city to which I have carried you into exile."

A prime example of the subversive power of these courageous Roman Christians was their response to the fifteen-year epidemic beginning in AD 165 that killed up to a third of the empire's population. During the reign of Marcus Aurelius, five thousand people a day were dying in Rome. This necessitated caravans of carts and wagons to haul the dead from the city. Doctors, priests, and nobles fled infected areas in droves, and even the famous physician Galen fled Rome itself as quickly as possible. But while pagans evacuated the city, Christians infiltrated it. They buried not just their own dead, but also pagans who had died without funds for a proper burial. They also supplied food, washed the sick, and consoled the dying. In short, these Christ followers were servant exiles making places of shalom in the midst of chaos, planting gardens in the midst of a devastated landscape, and acting as missionary doorkeepers beckoning hurting people to peace. Historian Charles E. Moore describes the powerful impact that Christians' faith had in Rome during those desperate days:

> Pagans could not help but notice that Christians not only found the strength to risk death, but through their care for one another they were much less likely to die. . . . In this way, the early Christians became, in the words of one scholar, "a whole force of miracle workers to heal the 'dying.'" Or as historian Rodney Stark puts it, "It was the soup [the Christians] so patiently spooned to the helpless that healed them." . . . The people of the Roman Empire were forced to admire their works and dedication. "Look how they love one another" was heard on the streets.[8]

Bringing Good Faith through a Different War

"Seek the peace and prosperity of the city to which I have carried you into exile." That's what God urged His people to do long
ago, and I'm convinced He wants His church to do the same thing
now, right here in America. Like the early Christians in Rome,
He wants us to assume the posture of servant exiles and grateful
foreigners as we bless people with the restoration of shalom and
fight the good fight of faith. When that happens, we will engage
what David Brooks terms "a different culture war, one just as central to [our] faith and far more powerful in its persuasive witness,"
in which we "could be the people who help reweave the sinews of
society . . . who go into underprivileged areas and form organizations to help nurture stable families . . . who build community
institutions in places where they are sparse . . . who converse . . .
about the transcendent in everyday life . . . as messengers of love,
dignity, commitment, communion and grace."[9]

As American culture becomes more and more paganized by
the gods of sex, money, and power, people will find their idola-
try just as futile and sad and pathetic as did the ancient Romans
and Babylonians. Emptiness and dissatisfaction and despair and
brokenness will comprise the new normal, replacing any flitting
vestiges of joy and meaning and contentment yet left over from
Christendom in the culture. While that's a bleak outlook for those
far from God, it's a tremendous opportunity for Christ followers
eager to bring them close by showering them with compassion
and living out the gospel.

Our God-given calling as the church is not to take up arms
against our neighbors, but to wrap our arms around them. Our
mission as a pilgrim people is not to attack, but to embrace; not
to hate, but to heal; not to condemn, but to bless, living out the

gospel as servant citizens of heaven in exile on the earth. That's why I have publicly and officially retired from my civil disobedience culture war. And that's why the church I have been privileged to lead since 1987, Irving Bible Church (IBC), has not only considered David Brooks's "different culture war. . . more powerful in its persuasive witness," but sought to enter it by becoming truly countercultural. We've embraced our biblical identity as foreigners and exiles (in the land of giants), relished our Simon Birch subversive powerlessness, cherished our role as doorkeepers in the house of God, and sought to emulate our shalom place-making elder brothers and sisters who transformed the ancient Roman Empire. The heart of IBCers for our community is not to fight wars or build walls, but to plant gardens and throw dinner parties; not to hurl stones, but to become place-makers of peace and doorkeepers of grace in the city to which God has brought us.

Often imperfectly, but always enthusiastically, our children's ministry mentors and youth leaders and worship leaders and mission-trip participants do that. An IBC staffer does that as she mobilizes hundreds to be a part of "Fashion for Freedom" events to support My Refuge House (a shelter and school for girls rescued from sex trafficking in the Philippines). Also doing that are the volunteers for our SchoolWorks program in our city's poorest public schools, where IBC participants run the "Half Hour Hero" reading program, lunch buddies for at-risk kids, and teacher appreciation events. We regularly house homeless people on our campus through Family Promise and have drilled over six hundred life-saving fresh water wells in South Sudan through the IBC-launched ministry "Water is Basic."[10] So we seek "to serve as messengers of love, dignity, commitment, communion and grace"[11] by mentoring inner-city kids through our partnership with Mercy Street, helping to give women a way out of the sex industry through our partnership with New Friends New Life and assisting in providing safe haven for battered women and children through our partnership with Brighter Tomorrows and The Gatehouse.

Both Garden-Planters *and* Spiritual Warriors

It is in this way that Christian foreigners and exiles exercise subversive power by serving people far from God. They effectively put God's peaceable kingdom on display as a different and better way to live, not only in the world, but with God for the world; not in flaunting strength, but by offering grace. Shalom place-makers offer peace to a broken world, and in the offering there is transformation not through PACs and politics, but through love and compassion. But not right away, and not all by itself, because there is spiritual opposition in the land of giants to all servant exiles who are about the building of God's kingdom in this earthly realm. Their offer of the gospel of peace actually foments spiritual warfare with the evil one. So Peter warns his beloved foreigners and exiles, "Be alert and of sober mind. Your enemy the devil prowls around like a roaring lion looking for someone to devour. *Resist him, standing firm* in the faith, because you know that the family of believers throughout the world is undergoing the same kind of sufferings" (1 Peter 5:8–9). Charles J. Chaput goes right to the reality of the settled spiritual resistance to God's peace plan experienced by Roman Christians two millennia ago as well as believers today: "Christians have many good reasons for hope. Optimism is another matter. Optimism assumes that, sooner or later, things will naturally turn out for the better. Hope has no such illusions."[12]

We Christians are indeed called to be shalom place-makers offering peace to a broken world, but we're never promised things will thereby naturally turn out for the better in the short run. Actually, as ancient Roman Christians discovered, just the opposite is true, as Peter had warned: "Who is going to harm you if you are eager to do good? But even if you should suffer for what is right, you are blessed. 'Do not fear their threats; do not be frightened'" (1 Peter 3:13–14). This opposition to those who live with a David faith in the truth of God's Word is the *spiritual warfare* that Paul references in encouraging a young pastor: "Timothy, my son, I am giving you this command in keeping with the prophecies once made about you, so that by recalling them you may *fight the battle well*, holding on to faith and a good conscience, which some have rejected and so have suffered shipwreck with regard to the faith" (1 Tim. 1:18–19).

> **The "good fight of faith" is a fight for truth against lies, for righteousness against evil, and for the innocent against aggressors.**

Only naïve optimism believes that ending culture wars and planting gardens alone will usher in spiritual peace in our broken world. Christians eschewing culture war does not and cannot mean forsaking spiritual warfare, which is the calling and burden of every Christian. As Paul exhorts Timothy:

> But you, man of God, flee from all this, and pursue righteousness, godliness, faith, love, endurance and gentleness. *Fight the good fight of the faith. . . .* Timothy, guard what has been entrusted to your care. Turn away from godless chatter and the opposing ideas of what is falsely called knowledge, which some have professed and in so doing have departed from the faith. (1 Tim. 6:11–12, 20–21)

The "good fight of faith" is a fight for truth against lies, for righteousness against evil, and for the innocent against aggressors. This battle is replete with Paul's dramatic invitation to young pastor Timothy (and through Timothy to us all): "You then, my son, be strong in the grace that is in Christ Jesus. . . . *Join with me in suffering, like a good soldier* of Christ Jesus" (2 Tim. 2:1, 3). In other words, love people well but also stand for often unpopular, offensive truth in the public square. Plant gardens and make places of peace but also defend yourself against the roaring lion who wants to end your witness and devour your life of faith. Let your light shine before others but also do not shrink back from protecting your family and your community from the onslaughts of flame-quenching evil. It's okay. You can and must be a place-maker of peace and a spiritual warrior at the same time.

> **Plant gardens and make places of peace but also defend yourself against the roaring lion who wants to end your witness and devour your life of faith. You can and must be a place-maker of peace and a spiritual warrior at the same time.**

That's precisely what our wonderful Roman elder brothers and sisters in the faith did back in the dark days of Nero's persecutions. Yes, they were place-makers of peace, but they also suffered for refusing to worship the Emperor as God, as well as for defying barbaric laws of exposure by rescuing infants (mostly female) left by callous parents to die as unwanted castaways. Yes, they ministered to the sick, but tradition says they also protected themselves from Roman persecutors by identifying themselves and their places of worship with the secret ichthys (fish) symbol.[13]

Like these courageous Christian forebears, God's peaceable soldiers today are called to fight the good fight of faith in the peculiarly righteous way described by Peter. "But in your hearts revere Christ as Lord. Always be prepared to give an answer to everyone who asks you to give the reason for the hope that you have. But do this with gentleness and respect, keeping a clear conscience, so that those who speak maliciously against your good behavior in Christ may be ashamed of their slander" (1 Peter 3:15–16).

Here is what Charles J. Chaput meant when he declared that, though optimism in the short run is an illusion, "Christians have many good reasons for hope."[14] The hope is that, as we plant gardens as place-makers of peace, we prosecute the spiritual warfare before us with firm gentleness and defend our faith and the truth with lucid reasonableness with the ultimate effect that "those who speak maliciously" against our good behavior in Christ "may be ashamed of their slander." That's what happened in fourth-century Rome when Emperor Constantine, having been riveted to the gospel message by the suffering of God's peaceable warriors over three centuries, elevated Christianity to be the dominant religion of the Roman Empire.[15] In their "powerful powerlessness," these early Roman believers were place-makers of peace, even as they fought the good fight of faith.

In our day, examples of Christians "giving an answer with gentleness and respect" to defend themselves against anti-faith giants in the land are the Christian family–owned Hobby Lobby[16] and the charitable order of nuns called the Little Sisters of the Poor.[17] Both groups fought the good fight of faith and truth against the anti-life requirements being forced upon them by the Affordable Care Act. They fought, the nation heard their gentle and respectful rebuttal, and autocratic government officials ultimately had occasion to be ashamed of their slander. In so doing, they

planted gardens even as they fought well the spiritual war waged
against them.

Do you know what God is giving to those who pursue His calling to plant gardens as foreigners and exiles and gentle warriors?
Courage. More courage than we've ever had. More than we've ever
experienced. As Henri Nouwen explains, this is the courage that
flows to those who are the beloved of our heavenly Father:

> As the Beloved of my heavenly Father, "I can walk in the
> valley of darkness: no evil will I fear." As the beloved . . . I can
> "give without charge," . . . confront, console, admonish, and
> encourage without fear of rejection or need for affirmation.
> As the Beloved, I can suffer persecution without desire for
> revenge and receive praise without using it as a proof of my
> goodness. As the Beloved, I can be tortured and killed with-
> out ever having to doubt that the love that is given to me is
> stronger than death. As the Beloved, I am free to live and give
> life, free also to die while giving life.[18]

All we are striving for is shalom. All we are seeking is the
chance to be place-makers of peace all over the place. All we are
attempting is to be agents of the new creation and doorkeepers of
grace. All we are doing is fulfilling God's call to plant gardens and
play the cello in our own neighborhoods and cities. As IBC Pastor
Ryan Sanders writes, "More and more church leaders are realizing that there is little difference between a post-Christian culture and a non-Christian culture. And there is a name for people
who are sent to deliver the good news to non-Christian cultures.
They're called missionaries. That is now the role of the practicing
American Christian. We are missionaries. Exiles."[19]

As servants and missionary and exiles then, let's find the courage to go farther up and further in. Intrepid are those who, from a posture of powerlessness, fight the good fight of faith and find their powerful God using them to transform the world. "Behold, how they love one another." Yes indeed! It's truly something to behold.

Section 2

GOD
ANOINTS US

1 SAMUEL 16:12–13

Then the LORD said, "Rise and anoint him; this is the one." So Samuel took the horn of oil and anointed him in the presence of his brothers, and from that day on the Spirit of the LORD came powerfully upon David.

THE IMPACT ON DAVID'S LIFE of being anointed by Samuel and thereby filled by the Holy Spirit of God was monumental. That experience was front and center for David when he penned his "last" words many years later.

> These are the last words of David: "The inspired utterance of David son of Jesse, the utterance of the man exalted by the Most High, the man anointed by the God of Jacob, the hero of Israel's songs: 'The Spirit of the LORD spoke through me. . . . When one rules over people in righteousness, when he rules in the fear of God, he is like the light of morning at sunrise. . . . If my house were not right with God, surely he would not have made with me an everlasting covenant, arranged and secured in every part; surely he would not bring to fruition my salvation and grant me my every desire.'" (2 Sam. 23:1–5)

David credits "the Spirit of the LORD" working in and through his life with every victory, every lasting benefit, every legendary accomplishment of his storied rule as king of Israel. How daunting must David's task have appeared to the young man when called by God from the sheepfold to the throne? Yet, in his own words as an old man, we see that having "the Spirit of the LORD come powerfully upon him" was the seminal event that bestowed the requisite courage David needed to fulfill his high calling.

And so it has ever been for God's people. To walk in the way of brave, they must lean on the anointing of God's Holy Spirit. As the great church father Tertullian wrote, "The Lord challenges us to suffer persecutions and to confess him. He wants those who belong to him to be brave and fearless. He himself shows how weakness of the flesh is overcome by courage of the Spirit. This is the testimony of the apostles and in particular of the representative, administrating Spirit."[1]

Chapter 3

THE WILD GOOSE

For the Spirit God gave us does not make us timid, but gives us power, love and self-discipline.—2 TIMOTHY 1:7

The Spirit you received does not make you slaves, so that you live in fear again; rather, the Spirit you received brought about your adoption to sonship. And by him we cry, "Abba, Father." —ROMANS 8:15

As filled with admiration as I am for David's *victory* in the Valley of Elah, I am even more filled with curiosity about David's *confidence* in entering that valley in the first place. It's surely impressive that (SPOILER ALERT!) David won the ensuing battle with Goliath. But it's even more impressive to me that he engaged the battle in the first place. No one else did, including the mighty men of Israel and even King Saul himself! Understandably, they were consumed with trepidation after enduring yet another of Goliath's verbal onslaughts replete I'm sure with grisly descriptions of what he planned to do to the various body parts of anyone foolish enough to fight him. Perhaps these men weren't physically shaking with fear, but they were clearly paralysis victims of the Goliath-generated dread that rendered them embarrassingly timid. Who can blame them? Facing an evil giant is enough to infect anyone with a bad case of the fainthearted jitters.

Surely the very confident (but also very human) David was

not immune to such phobia as he zigzagged his way down the valley's slope to the awaiting Goliath below. We know from Bilbo in
The Hobbit that courage is usually, if not always, accompanied by
knee-knocking fear: "'Go back?' he thought. 'No good at all! Go
sideways? Impossible! Go forward? Only thing to do! On we go!'
So up he got, and trotted along with his little sword held in front of
him and one hand feeling the wall, and his heart all of a patter and
a pitter."[1] No, David would not have been fearless. But he was un-
questionably intrepid. "Intrepid" derives from the Latin *intrepidus*,
itself formed by the combination of the prefix *in-* (meaning "not")
and *trepidus*, meaning "alarmed." Saul's and the soldiers' trepidation was apparent, yet David remained unalarmed. But why? For
the same reason that Frodo (in *The Lord of the Rings*) could stride
confidently toward danger though he too was scared—*he knew he
was not alone!* The inimitable Samwise Gamgee was Frodo's helper
every step of his courageous quest to Mordor. But as fabulous a
helper as Sam was, David's helper was (literally!) *infinitely* better,
because his Helper was none other than the third member of the
Holy Trinity.[2] Remember? "Then the LORD said, 'Rise and anoint
him; this is the one.' So Samuel took the horn of oil and anointed
him in the presence of his brothers, and from that day on *the Spirit
of the LORD* came powerfully upon David" (1 Sam. 16:12–13).

It was not long after this anointing that David, though surely
his heart was all a patter and a pitter, stood alone against Goliath,
because the Holy Spirit of the living God had come powerfully
upon him to construct a faith of the lamp-lighting, darkness-
illuminating, troop-running, wall-leaping (Ps. 18), and yes, giant-
slaying variety. Here's the best news yet. The Holy Spirit is eager
and willing to do the very same thing for you and me! "For the
Spirit God gave us does not make us timid, but gives us power,
love and self-discipline" (2 Tim. 1:7). The way to brave, then, for

us as it was for David, passes right smack through an anointing of our lives by the infilling presence of God's Holy Spirit. With His help we shall be brave! But if we're all alone in the land of giants, then we should plan to stay all jittery and paralyzed by trepidation along with Saul and the not-so-mighty-after-all men of Israel.

Trinitarians Again

I can hear your objections now (because I've expressed them already to myself), "What? *Plan* to live my life from a posture of retreat and fear? No way!" Who does that? Well, I have and perhaps you too if you've been as good-naturedly oblivious to the ministry the Holy Spirit wants to have in your life as I have through long seasons of my life. Oh, I've been theologically educated about the role of the Spirit in *the* Christian life even as I've often been experientially bereft of the power of said Spirit in *my* Christian life. That tends to happen when I slink back into my "go it alone" default lifestyle of self-sufficient, pull-yourself-up-by-the-bootstraps independence. Such foolishness prevailed until fifty years on the planet (and a gnarly cancer fight, which I'll tell you about shortly) finally and definitively taught me that I'm too dim for self-sufficiency, too weak for pull ups, and too stubborn for independence. "Whoa!" I learned. "I really *do* need help, and not only now. I always did (whether I realized it or not), and I always will!" Dare I suggest that you do too, my friend? Yes, you do too!

Perhaps this revelation is so hard-hitting to folks like us because we've been part of that vast swatch of Christendom that so often neglects the Spirit's work in our lives that He has become to us what Francis Chan calls the "Forgotten God."[3] Perhaps we have at times been so scared of falling into spiritual excesses (such as barking like dogs, "holy rolling," laughing uncontrollably, etc.) that we've neglected what Michael Horton terms "the shy member" of the Trinity[4] to the point of becoming practical "Binatarians" instead of biblical *Trinitarians*. Perhaps we've at times been so confused by the 1611 King James Bible designation of the Spirit as the "Holy Ghost" that we could personally confirm A. W. Tozer's famous point: when the average Christian thinks about the Holy Spirit "he is likely to imagine a nebulous substance like a wisp of invisible smoke which is said to be present in churches and to hover over good people when they die."[5] It's time that all of us now living in a Goliath world with a desperate need for a David faith to understand that the Holy Spirit is ever so much more than a benign ghost who hovers over good people. He is way more than a wispy poltergeist oft mistaken for smoke or a heavily mascaraed rock star. How silly. He is none of that! Rather, He is the Wild Goose . . .

The Holy Spirit (aka The Wild Goose)

Perhaps Irish DNA accounts for my love of the ancient Celtic Christian's description of God's Holy Spirit as "The Wild Goose" (*Ah Geadh-Glas* in Gaelic). That moniker should not surprise us, coming as it does from ancient Christians like Patrick (c. 390–460) and Columba (c. 521–597) whose faith is famed for its vitality and nurturing through flame and gale. These early believers saw how consistently Scripture paints the third member of the Trinity as completely untamable—a dynamic person represented by a dove but also by blazing fire and shredding wind, glorious and joyful and penetrating and just, well, *uncontrollable*. So they adopted a symbol for the Spirit that amped up the dove metaphor to what they considered its proper level of benign menace—"The Wild Goose"! I'm beholding right now a woven Celtic banner in my study (which I purchased at that Celtic treasure house, Trinity

College, Dublin) covered by a gaggle of beautiful, colorful, and by the look of them, *wild* geese. This is a modern piece representative of the work of ancient Celtic artists who regularly inscribed images of wild geese in their paintings and carvings on stone crosses and writings. They used the wild goose as a constant reminder that this static world of the material everywhere intersects the dynamic world of the Spirit in an almost magical way. Why that's important, Frederick Buechner explains:

> Here and there and not just in books we catch glimpses of a world of once upon a time and they lived happily ever after, of a world where there is a wizard to give courage and a heart, an angel with a white stone that has written on it our true and secret name, and it is so easy to dismiss it all. . . . But if the world of the fairy tale and our glimpses of it here and there are only a dream, they are one of the most haunting and powerful dreams that the world has ever dreamed.[6]

The Wild Goose is just that, a symbol used to inhabit a powerful dream that is not *only* a dream but also a true reality that produces what you and I desperately need: a David faith in a Goliath world.

> *Great Spirit, Wild Goose of the Almighty*
> *Be my eye in the dark places;*
> *Be my flight in the trapped places;*
> *Be my host in the wild places;*
> *Be my brood in the barren places;*
> *Be my formation in the lost places.*
> RAY SIMPSON[7]

My Host in the Wild Places

That's exactly what the Holy Spirit was to the freshly anointed David that day as he tripped and slid down the rocky north face of Elah Valley. Not a tame dove, but a wild goose. Not Luke Skywalker's impersonal "Force" to be manipulated Jedi-like in opposing an evil emperor, but David's powerful companion to be trusted in combatting an evil giant.[8] Is that why as the young shepherd approached Goliath (it's possible) he had a smile tugging at the corners of his mouth that astonished the hardened warriors of Israel, who thought grinning was a strange activity for a dead-man-walking? Was he sensing in that moment the Wild Goose functioning as his eye in the dark place, his flight in the trapped place, his host in the wild place that he was entering?

I think so. I think David was experiencing the reality of the powerful dream of the Wild Goose that Jesus would cast to His heartsick and fearful disciples eight hundred years later on the eve of His crucifixion. "If you love me, keep my commands. And I will ask the Father, and he will give you another advocate to help you and be with you forever—the Spirit of truth. The world cannot accept him, because it neither sees him nor knows him. But you know him, for he lives with you and will be in you" (John 14:15–17). This was fantastic

> If you're a Christ follower, He lives inside you and remains famously intolerant of an uninteresting status quo! Jesus didn't redeem us and send the Holy Spirit to us just to lead us gingerly on the path of safety, but to have this beautiful, Wild One lead us boldly striding in the way of brave.

news to Jesus' disciples, who knew that, up until then, almost the only individuals blessed with an anointing by the Holy Spirit were Israelite prophets, priests, and kings. But now Jesus was promising to everyone who follows Him the anointing of the same Spirit of truth that David had received. Finally! Thank You Jesus for Your substitutionary death and resurrection, making possible the anointing of Your Holy Spirit for *all* who believe!

Discerning disciples to this day should receive that great news with a whole kaleidoscope of butterflies in their stomachs because yes, we all get the same Spirit that David got, but remember, that's the Holy Spirit who led David to cheerfully engage an evil giant in single combat. Like C. S. Lewis's Aslan, the Goose is good, but He is not safe, and if you're a Christ follower, He lives inside you and remains famously intolerant of an uninteresting status quo! Jesus didn't redeem us and send the Holy Spirit to us just to lead us gingerly on the path of safety, but to have this beautiful, Wild One lead us boldly striding in the way of brave.

I Arise Today

So yes, there will be wild times following the Wild Goose, but let not your heart be troubled, because you'll never navigate them alone. Did you notice that Jesus calls the Spirit "another advocate" (John 14:16, literally "another of the same kind" as Christ, i.e., deity), which renders the Greek word "Paraclete," a word capable of such a large range of meanings (from "Helper" and "Advocate" to "Comforter" and "Counselor") that finding an English equivalent is difficult, as it was for the translators of the New Testament into the Karre language of equatorial Africa. How could they accurately render the "Paraclete" to that isolated people-group? One day the translators passed a group of porters carrying large bundles on their heads, with the exception of one, whom they assumed was the boss. However, they discovered he wasn't the boss. He just didn't carry a bundle because he had a special job. Should anyone faint with exhaustion, he would pick up the man's load and carry it for him. Hence that porter was known in the Karre language as "the one who falls down beside us." The translators had their words for "Paraclete"![9]

The beauty of having the third member of the Holy Trinity as our Paraclete is not just that He is our Helper, but that He is our ever-present Helper. As in constantly attentive. As in never absent. As in always available. That's why, on the eve of His crucifixion, Jesus told His disciples that they'd be worse off if He didn't leave them. "But very truly I tell you, it is for your good that I am going away. Unless I go away, the Advocate will not come to you; but if I go, I will send him to you" (John 16:7). Even though Jesus was (and is) the Son of God, He could only be in one place at one time because of the limitations of His humanity. So He wanted to ascend into heaven so that He could send the Holy Spirit to every believer as their ever-present, always-available Advocate. As Gordon Fee writes, "The living God is a God of power; and by the Spirit the power of the living God is present with us and for us."[10] Jesus sent the Spirit to be the power of the living God with us and for us. He sent the Spirit because He wanted to make it possible for all of His people to wholeheartedly pray with St. Patrick his wonderful AD 433 Celtic prayer (known as "St. Patrick's Breastplate") that he offered for divine protection on yet another of his "Wild Goose chases"[11] to convert the pagan Irish King Leoghaire to the faith. Here are some excerpts of the prayer that demonstrate Patrick's trust in the always-present Christ through Christ's ever-available Advocate and Paraclete:

I arise today / Through a mighty strength,
the invocation of the Trinity,
Through belief in the Threeness, / Through confession of the Oneness
of the Creator of creation.
I arise today / Through the strength of
Christ's birth with His baptism,
Through the strength of His crucifixion with His burial,
Through the strength of His resurrection with His ascension,
Through the strength of His descent for the judgment of doom . . .
I summon today . . . Christ to shield me
/ Against poison, against burning,
Against drowning, against wounding,
So that there may come to me an abundance of reward.
Christ with me, / Christ before me, / Christ behind me, / Christ in me,
Christ beneath me, / Christ above me, / Christ on my right,
/ Christ on my left,
Christ when I lie down, / Christ when I sit down,
/ Christ when I arise,
Christ in the heart of every man who thinks of me,
Christ in the mouth of everyone who speaks of me,
Christ in every eye that sees me, / Christ in every ear that hears me.[12]

A Better Kind of Wild Goose Chase

Now *there's* a powerful dream of a spiritual reality, that the in-dwelling, ever-available Holy Spirit of truth is like a Wild Goose falling down beside us to help when we enter lonesome valleys and face fearsome giants. That dream made David brave in a valley of fear. It made Jesus' disciples courageous in a Goliath world. And it made the apostle Paul and his team courageous through their many daunting ministry adventures on three major

missionary journeys into the land of giants. In writing to the believers at Corinth, notice how Paul gives credit to the Holy Spirit
for not only giving his team confidence, but also lasting spiritual
fruit in the perilous "Wild Goose chase" they'd completed.

> You show that you are a letter from Christ, the result of our
> ministry, written not with ink but with the Spirit of the living
> God, not on tablets of stone but on tablets of human hearts.
> Such confidence we have through Christ before God. Not
> that we are competent in ourselves to claim anything for our-
> selves, but our competence comes from God. He has made us
> competent as ministers of a new covenant—not of the letter
> but of the Spirit; for the letter kills, but the Spirit gives life."
> (2 Cor. 3:3–6)

Who knew, the Holy Spirit is a writer! His scroll is people's
lives, and His purpose is penning better stories for those lives.
That involves leading people on sometimes scary (though pur-
poseful, meaningful, and hopeful) Wild Goose chases in a Goliath
world, but He also shepherds and strengthens and comforts and
encourages them on the way as the *Paraclete* "who falls down
beside us," thus making the journey worth celebrating. David
stepped in behind the Holy Spirit and slew a giant, and Jesus' disciples followed the Spirit and established the church, and Paul's
guys pursued the Spirit in spreading the gospel throughout the
entire known world. Now those are what I call stories not written
with ink, but with the Spirit of the living God, not on tablets of
stone but on tablets of human hearts! Doesn't hearing about these
stories and their impact make your own heart yearn for the Spirit
to write such a "better story" of courage in your own life? It does
for me! And it does for Francis Chan, too.

It really is an astounding truth that the Spirit of Him who raised Jesus from the dead lives in you. He lives in me. I do not know what the Spirit will do or where He'll lead me each time I invite Him to guide me. But I am tired of living in a way that looks exactly like people who do not have the Holy Spirit of God living in them. I want to consistently live with an awareness of His strength. I want to be different today from what I was yesterday as the fruit of the Spirit becomes more manifest in me.

I want to live so that I am truly submitted to the Spirit's leading on a daily basis. Christ said it is better for us that the Spirit came, and I want to live like I know that is true. I don't want to keep crawling when I have the ability to fly.[13]

Neither do I. When we follow the Holy Spirit, we open our lives up to the His life-giving, kingdom-furthering, and God-glorifying adventures. How those chases look in each of our lives varies with our gifts, skills, callings, and context, but they are all equally exciting. For some, it may require moving overseas to join a mission agency in a remote African village, but for others it may mean taking up the charge in your current neighborhood to be salt and light, or maybe it means leading a small group or even volunteering at a homeless shelter. These are the "Wild Goose chases" we should pursue, not the purposeless, aimless searches for something that isn't there "wild goose chases" that we often find ourselves on. The temptation is to go after the aimless goose chases by searching for

> **When we follow the Wild Goose, we open our lives up to the Holy Spirit's life-giving, kingdom-furthering, and God-glorifying adventures.**

significance in a job, or in attaining renown, money, or certain relationships. But really we should be pursuing and going on the Spirit's "Wild Goose chases"—employing our gifts, serving the local church, and advancing the kingdom.

Boldly Traipsing from Strength to Strength

It was in July 2009 when the Lord tapped me on the shoulder and said He'd like me to follow the Wild Goose on a little adventure that would prove I should crawl no longer in my spiritual life and fly about everywhere instead. That adventure for me was also known as a diagnosis of stage IV colon cancer with only an 8-percent chance of survival. I'll be honest and admit it's not the faith-building adventure I would have selected had He been offering me choices. But He never does. He never asks if we want to venture. He just announces it's time to get going.

And so I did, Christ with me, Christ before me, Christ behind me, and Christ in me through innumerable scans and probes and tests. And so I did, Christ beneath me, Christ above me, Christ on my right, and Christ on my left through one minor and two (very) major surgeries. And so I did, Christ when I lie down, Christ when I sit down, and Christ when I arise through eighteen months of the most gnarly, neuropathy-producing, nausea-inducing, hair-ravaging, bodily-function interfering chemotherapy possible. Yes of course my heart was all of a patter and a pitter as I planned my own funeral and had the remarriage talk with my beloved Alice. But my trepidation constantly melted into an intrepid faith because the Spirit who had led me to this wild place was my *eye in the dark places and my flight in the trapped places and my host in the wild places and my brood in the barren places and my formation in the lost places* so much so that, in the big fat middle of that valley of pain I could "arise today through a mighty strength" and write these words from my heart:

> I have found that faith in this Valley draws one into a world shorn of fearful caution. While I battle the physical scourge of cancer, the life of faith teems with thrills, boldness, danger, shocks, yes some reversals, but also triumphs and epiphanies. For the first time in my life, I find myself relating to the apostle Paul whom I behold in Scripture boldly traipsing through the known world while contemplating risky trips to what must have seemed the antipodes (Spain), shaking the dust from his sandals and worrying not about the morrow, but only the moment. I dare to imagine that's how it was for him then, so it is for me (and you) now. We are embarking on no safe journey here, but it promises not to bore.[14]

I had discovered that the same Holy Spirit who leads us on hair-raising adventures also provides us peace on the journey. I had discovered that He is not safe, but He is wonderfully good and a Helper extraordinaire who is always there making courageous the hearts of those who willingly go on Wild Goose chases as pilgrims according to the joyful promises of Psalm 84: "Blessed are those whose strength is in you, whose hearts are set on pilgrimage. As they pass through the Valley of Baka, they make it a place of springs; the autumn rains also cover it with pools. They go from strength to strength, till each appears before God in Zion" (Ps. 84:5–7).[15]

There's only one way to go from strength to strength, and that's to heed the call of the Holy Spirit. There's only one way to turn trepidation with hearts all of a pitter and a patter into a David faith in our Goliath world, and that's to follow Him "out beyond the shore into the waves."[16]

The way to brave is following close the wake of the Paraclete as He plows the waves before us and falls down beside us. With the Spirit, our voyage is no less adventurous. The wind is still strong and the waves crest high and hearts still pitter and patter, but the Holy Spirit makes intrepid, unalarmed, and brave all who follow close in His train.

Chapter 4

CATCH THE WIND

The goal of Christian spirituality is to be enlivened by God's Spirit.
—Tony Jones, *The Sacred Way*

How to live in and by the Spirit is the single most important lesson
a believer can ever learn. —Robert Mounce

When young David received the anointing of God's Holy Spirit by the hand of Samuel the prophet, he suddenly enjoyed a dynamic personal relationship with the third member of the Holy Trinity. As we've learned, this Spirit was dubbed "The Wild Goose" by the Celts. But He is described by Jesus as a penetrating wind. "The wind blows wherever it pleases. You hear its sound, but you cannot tell where it comes from or where it is going. So it is with everyone born of the Spirit" (John 3:8). The word "Spirit" (*ruach* in Hebrew, *pneuma* in Greek, *spiritus* in Latin) means primarily "breath" or "wind." Jesus says "the wind" is uncontrollable. We hear the sound but don't know where it comes from or where it goes. It's free and powerful and far beyond human control. So it is with everyone born and matured by the Holy Spirit, through whose life the winds of God are blowing.

For David, this meant that he had a role to play in experiencing the power of the Spirit in his life. His anointing had not magically changed him into a robotic giant-slaying powerhouse. Rather, it simply offered him the invitation to "catch the wind" of the Spirit by trimming the sails of his soul. On the day David fought Goliath, his older brother Eliab chided him for his audacity in challenging the giant. But he totally misunderstood what was happening. David was not climbing a ladder. He was riding the wind. Attentive to the *ruach* of God in him, David wasn't charting his own course, but obediently coming about to God's course with the sure conviction that where the wind of the Spirit blew him, the power of God would accompany him.

David's anointing had not magically changed him into a robotic giant-slaying powerhouse. Rather, it simply offered him the invitation to "catch the wind" of the Spirit by trimming the sails of his soul.

That's God's invitation to the way to brave for all of us as well. Sure, it is a bit disconcerting that the direction of an unpredictable Spirit is the sweet spot of obedience for us as God's children. It would just seem safer to harness an outboard motor instead of the wind of the Holy Spirit in the land of giants! But as Frederick Buechner says, if we will follow David's example in riding the wind, we might find ourselves feeling more secure and more whole than ever before. "It is our business, as we journey, to keep our hearts open to the bright-winged presence of the Holy Ghost within us and the kingdom of God among us until little by little compassionate love begins to change from a moral exercise . . . into a joyous, spontaneous, self-forgetting response to the most real aspect of all reality, which is that the world is holy because God made it and so is every one of us as well . . . To live out of and toward that reality is little by little to become whole."[1]

Three postures are required to live out of and toward that reality: *poor in spirit*, *ceaseless prayer*, and *metamorphosis*.

Poor in Spirit

I'll never forget the inimitable Dr. Howard Hendricks asking us Dallas Theological Seminary students in class one day, "Do you think living a Christian life is easy or hard?" We all chimed in on the "hard" side, which brought a smile to his face as he corrected us all: "Living the Christian life is not hard. It's *impossible!*" As G. K. Chesterton commented, "Christianity has not been tried and found wanting; it's been found difficult and not tried." Christianity is not only difficult, but impossible when attempted in our own strength. It is a supernatural calling. That's why we mere mortals are wise to discern and acknowledge that we all desperately need God's help. When we do, Jesus famously pronounces us blessed! "Blessed are the poor in spirit, for theirs is the kingdom of heaven" (Matt. 5:3). Or, in The Message paraphrase, "You're blessed when you're at the end of your rope. With less of you there is more of God and his rule." How counterintuitive. At the end of my rope . . . *that's* when I attain the kingdom? Yes indeed.

Listen carefully to what Jesus says. We are not blessed by trying to become poor in spirit, but by recognizing that we already are. The word "poor" is the Greek *ptochos*, a beggar who lives off the alms of others. Jesus isn't recommending low self-esteem or pseudo-humility. Rather, He is recommending a sane sense of where we all stand spiritually in relation to a holy God. The poor in spirit recognize their true condition before God as spiritual "have nots." They don't have enough faith. They don't have enough strength. They don't have enough understanding. The poor in spirit are grateful for hope, but long to have more.

They try to obey, but realize their efforts consistently fall short. The poor in spirit, in other words, are needy, and they know it. They need God. They're dependent on Him. They're desperate for Him. As the great reformer John Calvin wrote, "He only who is reduced to nothing in himself, and relies on the mercy of God, is poor in spirit."

How is it that being reduced to nothing in ourselves and being cast on the mercy of God is a blessing? Because it clears out human pride and makes room for the Lord Himself on the throne of our hearts. Max Lucado, in his book *The Applause of Heaven*, writes,

> The jewel of joy is given to the impoverished spirits, not the affluent. God's delight is received upon surrender, not awarded upon conquest. The first step to joy is a plea for help, an acknowledgment of moral destitution, an admission of inward paucity. Those who taste God's presence have declared spiritual bankruptcy and are aware of their spiritual crisis. Their cupboards are bare. Their pockets are empty. Their options are gone. They have long since stopped demanding justice; they are pleading for mercy. They don't brag; they beg.[2]

That would not seem a happy outcome but for the fact that it's God to whom the poor in spirit beg, and it's only what God gives that the poor in spirit receive. History shows the Holy Spirit extremely capable of great gift-giving to those who acknowledge they have nothing.

Pastor Richard Wurmbrand was for fourteen years a Christian prisoner of conscience in a dark, communist prison cell underneath the city streets of Bucharest, Romania. He and his Christian brothers held there communicated by tapping on a sewer pipe that joined their isolation cells. As the weeks of captivity wore on,

Wurmbrand and his friends longed to share a Communion service together, but they had nothing. No church building. No beautiful music. No bread or wine. How could they have Communion with nothing?

"But wait," one of his friends tapped to Wurmbrand. "Nothing has to be something or you wouldn't have it. And consider, God hung the world on nothing! It has to be the strongest substance in the world." So with nothing in their hands, these prisoners broke bread. With nothing on their lips, they sipped from the cup. With reverent taps on a rusty sewer pipe, they worshiped the God of their salvation. In later years, Wurmbrand would remember many Communions, but none richer or sweeter than the one he celebrated with nothing at all.

But then in 1991, eighty-seven-year-old Richard Wurmbrand returned to post-revolution Bucharest, where jubilant believers gave him a tour of their new store—the first Christian bookstore in Bucharest in living memory. They took him to an underground room stuffed with Bibles and books and church supplies including Communion wafers and cups. As he peered into the little room, a look of puzzlement came over the old man's face. Then shock. Then boundless joy. That little room was the actual cell where he had spent fourteen years of his life. The very place where once he had shared Communion with no wine or bread was now a storehouse of plenty overflowing with God's Word, God's comfort, and God's exhortation. Though crippled in his feet from years of torture, Richard Wurmbrand danced for joy in realizing that when a man, woman, or child brings their nothing and yet offers it to God, God takes it very seriously indeed.[3]

He certainly did for David. What did that young shepherd have to offer God in the fight against Goliath that day long ago? A picnic basket and the scorn of his brothers. That's all. In other

> **David's acknowledging his poverty was the very key to gaining God's plenty. Hence the primary posture of one who would catch the wind of the Spirit is poverty of spirit.**

words, nothing. David was poor in spirit, and he knew it (we will see more evidence of this in chapter 5), and it pleased God to no end because David's acknowledging his poverty was the very key to gaining God's plenty. Hence the primary posture of one who would catch the wind of the Spirit is poverty of spirit. All of us are spiritually bankrupt in ourselves, hopeless unless God intervenes. But God rejoices when we acknowledge our need. "The poor in spirit are blessed because they have come to the end of their efforts to make it on their own and, having failed, are no longer too proud to admit it. They are desperate . . . poverty of spirit is the end of denial."[4]

I am one who struggles constantly with denial. What about you? I tend to drift constantly from "poor in spirit" toward "middle class" in spirit (as Tim Keller says)! I start feeling my oats, enjoying my successes, and thinking maybe it's time to start denying my poverty after all. It is then that God graciously knocks the stuffing out of me through failure or trials or burdens far too heavy for me to carry. These serve as loving reminders that without Him, I have nothing, but when we bring our nothing and offer it to God, He takes it very seriously. I recently admitted as much in a recent sermon when I shared with my friends my regular, pre-sermon prayer. It's not, "Lord, speak through me," though that would be a very strategic prayer. It's not, "Let Your Word go out powerfully today," though that would be an appropriately results-oriented prayer. Rather, my regular pre-sermon prayer is not strategic or results-oriented, just authentically needy. What I do say is, "Lord, I 'got' nothin'." If the Spirit doesn't show up and the Wild Goose hold forth and the Comforter wax eloquent, I can't put one word in front of another to any true spiritual effect. I've learned that if I don't catch the wind of the Spirit, I might as well hang it up for the day. In and of myself, I got nothin'. But I've also learned that when I ask, the Spirit responds consistently and lovingly and powerfully. Which brings us to prayer . . .

Pray Without Ceasing

Paul the apostle gives us the second great principle of "catching the wind" in the following simple but profound exhortation: "Rejoice always, pray without ceasing, give thanks in all circumstances; for this is the will of God in Christ Jesus for you" (1 Thess. 5:16–19 ESV). How can we avoid quenching and stay in step with the Spirit? Pray. And when we've prayed, we pray some more as naturally as we breathe some more. As Jim Cymbala notes, this is what the early church leaders did: "In Acts 4, when the apostles were unjustly arrested, imprisoned, and threatened, they didn't call for a protest; they didn't reach for some political leverage. Instead, they headed to a prayer meeting. Soon the place was vibrating with the power of the Holy Spirit (vv. 23-31). The apostles had this instinct: When in trouble, pray. When intimidated, pray. When challenged, pray. When persecuted, pray."[5] From David's prayers in the Psalms, we see that the apostles were only following suit. The courage they derived from heartfelt prayers to God through the Holy Spirit was just a reflection of the courage David derived from heartfelt prayers to God through the Holy Spirit in the Valley of Elah.

Their todays were unsteady and their tomorrows obscure. Their times were desperate and therefore their prayers too, much more so I suspect than ours today because brevity of life was a given.

Eight hundred years after the apostles, my beloved Celts followed suit with heartfelt prayers to God through the Holy Spirit, as much out of desperation as aspiration. In their corner of Europe, infant mortality was as high as life was short, and leprosy and the plague were common. Medicine was rare and hospitals not yet. Their todays were unsteady and their tomorrows obscure. Their times were desperate and therefore their prayers too, much more so I suspect than ours today because brevity of life was a given. As the late great theologian and poet Calvin Miller observed,

> God stirs the ashes of your old hopes when you have faced the fact that your lifespan, like that of the Celts, is short. But your prayers endure forever. None of them die. They live in the air about you and they move us like the breeze of Pentecost. They may appear dead, but they sometimes lay like an ember in the dull, gray ash of the present moment. Then the Spirit blows, the coals flare and the fire burns hot. Even now, the Celtic embers of spirituality are catching fire all around us.[6]

One of the main forms of prayer practiced by the Celts was the "lorica." The lorica is a breastplate. The "loricae" of the Celts were their prayers calling on God to protect them with His grace. For example, Patrick's "Breastplate" (in the last chapter) was a lorica. Hear his testimony: "I was like a stone lying in the deepest mire; and then, he who is mighty came, and, in his mercy, raised me up. He most truly raised me on high and set me on top of the rampart." Then that great Irish saint prayed this lorica: "Lord, set me on the rampart. Give me health enough to live to complete the dream."[7] The Spirit responded to Patrick's prayer, and those pagan Irish were miraculously transformed by the power of God.

In *Foundation*, our discipleship experience at IBC, we teach people to pray daily, "Holy Spirit, I am weak. You are strong. Be strong in me." This is a simple lorica that has transformed my (and many others') waking hours into long-running conversations with God. I think it did so for my dear mother before she passed away just a few years ago. When she was at life's end, Alice and I flew to North Carolina to be with my mother as she suffered the final stages of ALS. One day as we left her hospital room, I cleared some used pages to make room on her writing pad (she could no longer speak and suffered from dementia, but she could still write) and stuck them in my Bible. On the airplane home, here's what I read in my mom's strong, clear hand from 11/8/14:

Please help me Jesus, I don't want to be alone. I miss my family. Eric and I had three sons, Andy, Tim, and Phil. Andy lives in Texas with his family. Tim lives in NC with his family. And Phil lives in N. Va with his family . . . Amazing grace, how sweet the sound that saved a wretch like me. Amazing pity, grace unbound, and love beyond degree . . . I want to get a good night's rest. Please help me to do this, Jesus. Help me to feel better. Help me to relax and get a deep breath and to get to sleep soon. I am so tired. Please Jesus, help me to get a good night's rest. These people are so good to me. I thank you for each one of them! . . . Jesus loves me, this I know. For the Bible tells me so. Little ones to Him belong. They are weak but He is strong. Yes, Jesus loves me. Yes, Jesus loves me. Yes,

Jesus loves me, the Bible tells me so. And I believe what the Bible says!

My mother's mind was burdened, but her spirit soared. She was facing a fearful passage from this life to the next, but she did so with a grateful heart and an intrepid soul. How? Through living moment by moment in the power and comfort of prayer. In these few words (and there were many more pages full of them) scribbled on paper, my mother honestly expressed her fear and pain. But she did so not in despair, but with faith, hope, and love. My too proud heart is just shredded by her courage and strength in those final hours of her life, when true courage and strength simply could not be faked. Mom knew she was weak. But she also knew the Holy Spirit is strong. So she asked Him to be strong in her, and He was, just like He was for David and for St. Patrick, and just like He will be for you and me as well.

Metamorphosis

The third main posture God has given His children for effectively catching the wind of the Holy Spirit is metamorphosis. God's goal for all His children is that they change *from the inside out*. God's ultimate destination for all of us is that we become like Jesus, who is the very definition of spiritual maturity. "For those God foreknew he also predestined to be conformed to the image of his Son, that he might be the firstborn among many brothers and sisters" (Rom. 8:29). Such Jesus *conformation* constitutes character *transformation*, which requires spiritual *formation*. The good news according to the apostle Paul is that spiritual formation is the Holy Spirit's specialty in the lives of all Christ followers. "So I say, walk by the Spirit, and you will not gratify the desires of the flesh" (Gal. 5:16). Spiritual formation is the process of establishing the character of Christ in a person through the power of the Holy Spirit and under the direction of God's Word.

That sounds simpler in theory than in execution. In actuality, sanctification is a long, hard slog that requires faithful focus and perseverance. The inherent difficulty in keeping in step with the Spirit causes many believers (including myself!) to fall into the "Yoga Poseur" mentality. A few years ago, a *Wall Street Journal* article entitled "Yoga Poseurs" asks, "Why work out when you can just buy the clothes and look like you did?"[8] Christ followers who back away from the discipline of staying in step with the Spirit are like spiritual Yoga Poseurs. I find when I enter that space that I'm not asking the growth question, "What kind of person does God want me to be?" but the poseur's question, "What kind of person can I pretend to be?" I start focusing on external stuff that others see, not on my heart, which only God sees.

Repelled by yoga-poseur spirituality, many of us believers grit our teeth and determine (again!) to gut out sanctification by sheer effort and willpower. We will just try harder to do better! But this too is futile, because try as we might, we can't transform ourselves. I can grunt and strain and attempt mightily to have a better temper, more patience, and more love for people. I can try mightily not to get waylaid by lust, pounded by pride, and shanghaied by selfishness. But it won't work. True Christian character is the fruit of the Spirit. You can't produce it by straining and grunting and trying hard. Want the fulfillment of holiness? That's good. The Holy Spirit wants that for you, too. Want to be growing more like Jesus with every passing day? Wonderful. He wants that for you, too. Want to live your life to the fullest and experience the power of God? Great. He wants that for you, too. But He also wants you to know that you can't do any of this alone. Holiness involves more

If God can change a long, squishy creature with a lot of legs into a graceful, colorful creature with wings, don't you believe He can change an ornery person into a sweet one, a selfish person into a servant-hearted one, a lazy person into a disciplined one, an alienated, unloving person into a reconciled one, a lewd person into a pure one, or a Yoga poseur into a fully devoted follower of Christ?

than trying; it involves transformation, and transformation is a supernatural occurrence that only happens in our lives through the Holy Spirit of God: "Now the Lord is the Spirit, and where the Spirit of the Lord is, there is freedom. And we, who with unveiled faces all reflect the Lord's glory, are being transformed into his image with ever-increasing glory, which comes from the Lord, who is the Spirit" (2 Cor. 3:17–18).

The word *transformed* here is a translation of the Greek verb *metamorphoo*, from which we get the word *metamorphosis*. For instance, in the species *samia cecropia* of the order Lepidoptera, one of God's greatest miracles of change occurs with continuous regularity, and it's a process that you know all about! The order Lepidoptera consists of moths and butterflies, and *samia cecropia* is better known as a silkworm. In its lifetime, the cecropia moth begins as an egg, hatches into a larva, which becomes a caterpillar that molts its skin four times as it grows. Then it spins a cocoon and enters the pupa stage for winter. But springtime brings the most incredible transformation. What began as an egg, became a worm, and spent the winter as a pupa, now emerges as a fully developed moth. Scientists can describe this process in detail, but they can't explain it; they know what happens, but not why. It is one of God's miracles of change. It is the wind. It is metamorphosis. It is what the Holy Spirit does.

If metamorphosis is a credible miracle for worms, why not for people? If God can change a long, squishy creature with a lot of legs into a graceful, colorful creature with wings, don't you believe He can change an ornery person into a sweet one, a selfish person into a servant-hearted one, a lazy person into a disciplined one, an alienated, unloving person into a reconciled one, a lewd person into a pure one, or a Yoga poseur into a fully devoted follower of Christ? It may appear as monumental a task as moving mountains, but never fear, that's God's business! Our job is not to make the wind blow, but just to raise high our sails to catch the wind of the Spirit as He "morphs" us! Again, Paul explains this process. "And we all, who with unveiled faces contemplate the Lord's glory, are being transformed into his image with ever-increasing glory, which comes from the Lord, who is the Spirit" (2 Cor. 3:18).

Contemplating the Lord's glory is simply paying attention to His glory by practicing three fundamental spiritual disciplines of the Christian life: Word, Prayer, and Community. What is the *object* of our contemplation? The truth of God's Word! What is the *expression* of our contemplation? The passion of our prayer! What is the *context* of our contemplation? The community of our brothers and sisters in Christ! So what are we doing when daily we contemplate the Lord's glory and pay attention to His work in our lives by digesting His Word and bending His ear and loving His people? We're not changing ourselves, just raising our sails. We're not "earning our keep," just catching the wind. "For what the law was powerless to do because it was weakened by the flesh, God did by sending his own Son in the likeness of sinful flesh to be a sin offering. And so he condemned sin in the flesh, in order that the righteous requirement of the law might be fully met in us, who do not live according to the flesh but according to the Spirit" (Rom. 8:3–4).

So don't redouble your efforts.[9] Just trim your sails. Don't obsess about your inevitable failures, but simply embrace (gratefully!) the Spirit's triumphs. Do it prayerfully, with poverty of spirit, and with the anticipation of metamorphosis. If you do, you will find with David that the resulting transformation in your life is the way to brave. Remember his meditation in Psalm 18? Catching the wind of the Spirit in his life was like a shield of refuge for David, metamorphosing his "darkness to light" and giving him the courage to "run against a troop" and the strength to "leap over a wall." It will do the same for us as well if only we will determine to trim our sails. So let's do so, shall we? We will need to if we are to successfully navigate the next stop on the way to brave.

Section 3

GOD
BREAKS US

1 SAMUEL 16:10–11

Jesse had seven of his sons pass before Samuel, but Samuel said to him, "The LORD has not chosen these." So he asked Jesse, "Are these all the sons you have?" "There is still the youngest," Jesse answered. "He is tending the sheep."

A TRADITIONAL JEWISH HISTORY teaches that David was an illegitimate son of Jesse and therefore a reminder of shame and carrier of scorn.[1] Is this why David's famous Psalm 51 prayer of repentance notes that "in sin did my mother conceive me" (KJV)? Is this why David, like Cinderella, was less loved by his parent than his half-siblings and left behind to ignominious tasks while they got to experience an exciting field trip to hang with the handsome prince and his crew? I think so. And I believe all this pain was God's blessing in disguise to David because it broke his pride early and compelled him to put his faith in God.

So David's pride was broken early, and his resulting humble desire that God get all glory gave him confidence that, even though he had to face Goliath, it was really just him facing Goliath on God's behalf. Knowing he was weak but God was strong made David brave. And it will also make Christians and churches brave as we simultaneously embrace our brokenness and pursue God's glory.

Chapter 5

CRUCIBLE AND CHARACTER

It is doubtful whether God can bless a man greatly
until He has hurt him deeply. —A. W. Tozer

Behold, I have refined thee, but not with silver; I have chosen
thee in the furnace of affliction. —Isaiah 48:10 KJV

David's upbringing as the youngest of six sons is the consummate
Old Testament Cinderella story. A fundamental but often over-
looked element of this beloved tale is the part about the "cinders."
We love to pour scorn on the favoritism of self-centered parents
and the cruel self-absorption of arrogant siblings. We love to root
for the courageous "Cinderella" herself and to celebrate her come-
uppance. Yet we don't love to recognize the difficult, character-
shaping season of cinders as a good and necessary element in
Cinderella's progression toward donning the glass slipper.

But we should, because the character shaped in the crucible
of cinders is the basis for later greatness. Without pain, suffering,
and brokenness melting away the dross of self-sufficiency and
pride in our lives, we see no real need for the power of God to work
through our lives. The result is diminished Christian courage because as unbroken and completely self-reliant people, we talk

ourselves into believing that our own limited, individual strength is sufficient though knowing all the while that it is not. Eugene Peterson refutes this dangerous self-deception: "Individualism is the growth-stunting, maturity-inhibiting habit of understanding growth as an isolated self-project. Individualism is self-ism with a swagger. The individualist is the person who is convinced that he or she can serve God without dealing with God."[1] All who yearn for a David faith in a Goliath world must be disabused of that misunderstanding. Want to serve God courageously? Then you must deal with God, and that means God dealing with your pride.

The Problem of Pride

Yes, pride really is our problem, and a very big problem indeed. According to the apostle Peter, it sets the Almighty against us. "God opposes the proud" (1 Peter 5:5). Not to belabor the obvious—but the very last Person in the universe we want to make our adversary is God! But history shows that's precisely the fruit of human pride. Pride first showed up in the Bible in the garden of Eden when Satan, embodied as a snake, told Eve, "When you eat this fruit, your eyes will be opened, and you'll be like God" (see Gen. 3:5). The snake appealed to Eve's pride, and it worked. "I'll be master of my own universe. I won't have to submit to anybody else's rules. I can just be my own God." Here is the central problem with pride. It is not just that it "makes it all about me," but that it leaves God right out of the picture.

Pride makes us fancy ourselves—not God, the source of all good things—capable of all great things. That's why "arrogance" is a good synonym for pride. Its root is in the verb "arrogate," which is to claim for ourselves that which is not rightly ours. Arrogant people position themselves squarely in the center of their own universe as they revel in an unholy preoccupation with themselves. The prevalence of human pride led one astute observer to point out, "The biggest difference between you and God is God doesn't think he's you."

Psychologists call this prideful assumption of limitless personal capability "illusory superiority." (It's also called the "Lake Wobegon Effect," from Garrison Keillor's fictional Minnesota town where "all the children are above average.") Studies show that we humans tend to inflate our positive qualities in comparison to others. Christian psychologist Mark McMinn summarized the data: "It's the great contradiction: the average person believes he is a better person than the average person." He contends that the "Lake Wobegon Effect" is nothing more than human pride. "One of the clearest conclusions of social science research is that we are proud. We think better of ourselves than we really are, we see our faults in faint black and white rather than in vivid color, and we assume the worst in others while assuming the best in ourselves."[2] And that's not all. Dr. Sukhvinder Obhi, a neuroscientist at McMaster University in Ontario, recently put the heads of a number of powerful people under a transcranial-magnetic-stimulation machine. He found that the acquisition of power with its sidekick pride actually impairs a specific neural process called "mirroring," which is the cornerstone of empathy. Obhi describes it "as a sort of tumor that ends by killing the victim's sympathies."[3]

No wonder God is not a fan of our prideful human mindset. He made His reasons for opposing it abundantly clear to the Israelites

> **Pride transforms our lives into monuments of self-reliance, tiny, personal universes from which God has been squeezed out.**

in the Old Testament. Having finally completed their wearying laps around the wilderness, they peer over the border at the cushy Canaanite homes and manicured lawns that will soon be theirs. But before they enter, Moses warns them of a lurking danger.

> The LORD your God is bringing you into a good land . . . a land where bread will not be scarce and you will lack nothing . . . When you have eaten and are satisfied, praise the LORD your God for the good land he has given you. Be careful that you do not forget the LORD your God. . . . Otherwise . . . your heart will become proud and you will forget the LORD your God. . . . You may say to yourself, "My power and the strength of my hands have produced this wealth for me." But remember the LORD your God, for it is he who gives you the ability to produce wealth. . . . If you ever forget the LORD your God . . . I testify against you today that you will surely be destroyed. (Deut. 8:7–19)

Israel is facing a danger more destructive than starvation, heat stroke, or scorpion bite. The enemy? A spiritual disease called pride. Pride is amnesia of the soul. It is forgetting God. It is self-regarding self-sufficiency. Pride transforms our lives into monuments of self-reliance, tiny, personal universes from which God has been squeezed out. Sure, we believe in Him. But actively rely on Him? Nah. Pride is acting—whether we openly deny Him or merely ignore Him—as though we have no need of God. It is not merely an inflated ego; it is an inflated soul.

God doesn't like that, not even a little bit. In fact, He actively opposes it! *The Winner's Curse* is the name of a book by economist Richard Thaler, who studied gamblers in Las Vegas and found their greatest losses usually followed their greatest wins. Believing they were gambling geniuses, they unwisely bet huge stakes only to lose everything. Thaler concluded that our greatest successes can produce in us selfish pride that serves as a prelude to our worst failures. As ancient wisdom predicts, "Pride goes before destruction, a haughty spirit before a fall" (Prov. 16:18). Make no mistake, God is the author of that inevitable sequence. What social scientists call "the winner's curse" is God's resistance to human illusory superiority. And that's why pride is such a huge impediment to the way of brave. It cuts us off from the source of true courage.

Gratefully Broken

Counterintuitively, one of the greatest gifts God can give to a Christian individualist is an all-expense-paid stint in the crucible of character. It's there alone where we stubborn, self-confident individualists can be disabused of our silly, destructive notions of prideful self-sufficiency. As Gordon MacDonald writes, "What will it take to force us into disciplined cultivation of the inner garden of our private worlds? Will it require an experience of severe suffering? That is what history seems to say over and over again: those under pressure seek God, because there is nothing else. Those smothered in 'blessings' tend to drift with the current. And that is why I question the word blessing sometimes. Surely something is not a blessing if it seduces us away from inward spiritual cultivation."[4] Before we can be truly blessed, therefore, we must be deeply broken. Our character must be forged in the crucible of pain, suffering, and brokenness because that's where God replaces the dross of self-sufficiency and pride in our lives with His own mighty power. Until pride is broken, power cannot flow.

This is Jacob's story in the Old Testament. He was broken, but not resentfully or bitterly broken. Seeing that God's blessing and power flowed from his pain, he was gratefully broken. Jacob was on his way home from his Uncle Laban's house in Haran to Canaan, where finally he had to face the wrath of his wronged brother Esau, whose birthright he had stolen. "That night Jacob got up and took his two wives, his two female servants and his eleven sons and crossed the ford of the Jabbok" (Gen. 32:22).

On this night before their encounter, God brought Jacob to a place of isolation for a confrontation that produced desperation and resulted in transformation! For fourteen years, Jacob had stoked his pride by acquiring what he wanted through deceptive cleverness. But now God was going to put an end to that streak by breaking Jacob's pride in the crucible of pain. Jacob's song was, "I did it my way." God would answer, "Not any more." "After he had sent them across the stream, he sent over all his possessions. So Jacob was left alone, and a man wrestled with him till day-break. . . . The man asked him, 'What is your name?' 'Jacob,' he answered" (Gen. 32:23–24, 27).

Talk about X-Files, this is one strange story! Jacob is camping on the banks of the Jabbok River (literally "Wrestle" River, appropriately enough) when God jumps him. Like Cato on Peter Sellers in the iconic old Pink Panther movies, God appeared in human form and locked Jacob in the Von Eric death grip. The mysterious wrestler here is a theophany, an appearance of God in human form. But Jacob doesn't know who his adversary is, and he's not going to take this lying down! He counters Him with the Hulk Hogan Scissors hold, and an all-night "Wrestlemania" ensues.

When the man saw that he could not overpower him, he touched the socket of Jacob's hip so that his hip was wrenched as he wrestled with the man. Then the man said, "Let me go, for it is daybreak."

> But Jacob replied, "I will not let you go unless you bless me."
> The man asked him, "What is your name?"
> "Jacob," he answered. (32:25–27)

Jacob is exhausted—wouldn't you be if your wrestling opponent were the almighty God?! But he won't quit, so God "lightly touches" him and dislocates Jake's hip, the point of his greatest physical strength. The message is clear: even our greatest strengths are woefully inadequate when pitted against the will of God! When you wrestle with God, you always lose! Jacob suddenly catches on—this is no ordinary mugger. This is God! Incapacitated now and duly humbled, Jacob stops fighting God and implores His blessing. But before blessing Jacob, God insists that Jacob acknowledge who and what he really was—a despicable sinner in need of God's grace. "What is your name?" God asks. Did He not know Jacob? Of course He did. But part of the pain of breaking Jacob's pride was getting Jacob to admit the truth about himself. "Pain plants the flag of reality in the fortress of a rebel heart" (Anonymous). One's name represented one's character, and the meaning of Jacob's name described him to a tee: "Heel-grabber, deceiver, cheater." By this point in his life, Jacob had fully earned his handle! He was the prideful poseur of all poseurs, the prideful pretender of all pretenders, the prideful imposter of all imposters. God already knew this. He just wanted Jacob to acknowledge the sad truth. So he demanded to know, "Jacob, are you (finally!) ready to admit who you really are?" Jacob was. He broke and confessed, "I am Jacob."

Jacob's wrestling match is a spiritual parable of how God works in human hearts. Instead of vaporizing us for our sin, He wrestles with us through the vicissitudes of life, breaking us of our pride so that He can bless us with His power. F. B. Meyer puts

Jacob's wrestling match is a spiritual parable of how God works in human hearts. Instead of vaporizing us for our sin, He wrestles with us through the vicissitudes of life, breaking us of our pride so that He can bless us with His power.

it this way, "Whatever it is that enables a soul, whom God designs to bless, to stand out against Him, God will touch. It may be the pride of wealth; or of influence; or of affection: but it will not be spared—God will touch it. It may be something as natural as a sinew; but if it robs a man of spiritual blessing, God will touch it."[5]

"God will touch it." Not necessarily the wealth or the influence or the affection, but the *pride* anchored in those things. That's a kindhearted gesture from a loving heavenly Father, not a threat from a heartless ogre. Jacob needed God's touch, and would later be grateful for it all his life. Same with young David. The way the Bible describes him, David was a sitting duck for the ravages of pride and the inevitable downfall of illusory superiority and the winner's curse. Remember the prophet's physical description of the young David in 1 Samuel 16:12? "He was glowing with health and had a fine appearance and handsome features." Now put David's movie star mug alongside his other known attributes. He was powerfully athletic, a born leader, whip-smart, a practitioner of the poet's art, and played a mean electric guitar (or harp, rather). He was the ancient equivalent of a professional football player, rock star, thespian, and movie star all rolled into one. Talented, good-looking young buck like that, why even think he needed God? Pride goes before a fall (Prov. 16:18), and David had all the inducements to a world-class pride that would have precipitated a catastrophic fall before he ever got started.

That's why God mercifully, lovingly, and graciously broke David's pride and humbled him as an outcast, possibly illegitimate son relegated by a dismissive father to the sheepfold. God had big plans for David, and didn't want pride to make him fall. David's pride was broken early, and his resulting humble desire that God get all glory later gave him confidence that, even though he had to face Goliath, it was really just him facing Goliath on God's behalf. Knowing he was weak but God was strong made David dauntless. And it will also make Christians and churches brave as we embrace our brokenness and pursue God's glory.

One of my own personal seasons of painful, blessed breaking by "Wrestle River" began on October 7, 1986, with the emergency C-section birth of our third daughter Bonnie (whose due date was December 23!). My wife Alice had gone in for a routine prenatal checkup in which her doctor discovered she'd developed preeclampsia, a deadly condition in expectant mothers that produces dangerously high blood pressure that can only be lowered by the birth of the baby. Her pressure was so extreme that the doctor gently moved her to a prone position and quietly, calmly told her not to move until a nurse could grab a wheelchair and take her immediately to the hospital. He was terrified that she might stroke out and die right there in his office! I'll never forget him calling me at work from that very examination room to say that he needed to do an emergency C-section to save Alice's life. "But the baby," I said. "It's too early, isn't it?" The child (at that point, we didn't even know if our baby was a boy or girl) was due in late December. But I was talking to the doctor on October 7. I did the math. Two and a half months early? Ten weeks premature? "Could our baby even survive that C-section?" I asked. "I truly don't know," the doctor replied. "What I do know is that if we don't take the child right away, we may lose both mother and child before the day is out. What do you want to do?"

Thus began my own personal Jabbok River breaking experience. Just months before, I had graduated with high honors from Dallas Theological Seminary after helping plant a thriving young church during my four years of study. I was full of all kinds of theological vim (I still remembered all my Greek and Hebrew and systematic theology back then!) and vigor (I was a recognized young leader who was about to get my first call as a senior pastor to Irving Bible Church) and "feeling my oats" of success with relish. People looked to me for leadership and sought me out for answers, and that felt good. So good that I'd grown proud. Proud of what I knew and proud of what I could do and proud of where I was headed.

Then, unexpectedly, I'm fielding this most terrible question, this most breaking question I've ever been asked in my entire life. If we don't deliver this child, your wife could die. "What do you want to do?" But if we deliver almost three months early, this child will most likely die. "What do you want to do?" Suddenly, I realized that I knew nothing. I could do nothing. And I didn't know where to go. "What is your name now, Eric Andrew McQuitty?" whispered the Spirit of God. "Doc, we have to do the section" (this actually was one of those life-of-the-mother versus life-of-the-baby decisions that sometimes, even if rarely, have to be made). While I was hustling in to the hospital, the doctor ordered an ultrasound to see how big the baby was and discovered her gender. When I arrived, Alice and I spent a few tearful moments (while they were prepping her for surgery) coming up with our little girl's name. Bonnie Caroleen McQuitty. I called our church's prayer chain with Bonnie's name and then prepped for the operating theater so I could be at Alice's side during the surgery. While I scrubbed, I honestly answered the Spirit's question. "My name is Scared, Weak, Fearful, and Lost." And then it happened. "If it robs a man of spiritual blessing, God will touch it." My pride of achievement and self-sufficiency had me in great danger, and God graciously touched it and broke it for me in that moment.

The Cinderella part of Jacob's story came after "God touched it" for him. "Then the man said, 'Your name will no longer be Jacob, but Israel, because you have struggled with God and with humans and have overcome.' Jacob said, 'Please tell me your name.' But he replied, 'Why do you ask my name?' Then he blessed him there. So Jacob called the place Peniel, saying, 'It is because I saw God face to face, and yet my life was spared'" (Gen. 32:28–30).

Jacob didn't ultimately overcome in the crucible by exercising his strength, but by recognizing his weakness. God blessed Jacob not because he was triumphant, but because he became dependent. It wasn't when Jacob fought God that he prevailed, but when he "wept and begged for his favor" (Hos. 12:4).

When God changed Jacob's name, it was to reflect a change in Jacob's character. Jacob was now Israel. The Hebrew text here contains a great play on words. In the older versions, "Israel" is translated as "one who prevails with God," but literally it means the opposite, "God who prevails with man." Jacob didn't struggle with God and win; God struggled with Jacob and won! So what does "Israel" mean? It truly has a double meaning: God brought Jacob to a place of surrender, but in that surrender, Jacob was victorious. In losing, he won! Jacob didn't ultimately overcome in the crucible by exercising his strength, but by recognizing his weakness. God blessed Jacob not because he was triumphant, but because he became dependent. It wasn't when Jacob fought God that he prevailed, but when he "wept and begged for his favor" (Hos. 12:4). God refuses to yield to our strength, but He longs to be overcome by our repentance! Remember? "God opposes the proud but shows favor to the humble. Humble yourselves, therefore, under God's mighty hand, that he may lift you up in due time" (1 Peter 5:5–6).

"We too should cross the creek alone and struggle with God over ourselves," writes Max Lucado. "We too should stand eyeball to eyeball with him and be reminded that left alone we fail. We too should unmask our stained hearts and grimy souls and be honest with the One who knows our most secret sins."[6] But whether we do or not is a choice that only we can make. Did you notice that, in the wrestling match, the Lord never did pin Jacob? Could He have? Absolutely, but He never did. What does that tell us? God will never make you anything you don't want to be. He'll wrestle with you but never pin you. You're going to have to say "Lord,

> **Jacob had learned that it is better for us to limp through life leaning on God than to strut through life trusting in ourselves. Those whom God powerfully uses and courageously infuses are those who hobble across the finish line broken but invincible in God's strength.**

I'll not let you go, except you bless me." If you do, you will be able to share the story of Jacob's stint in the crucible of character that ends with a tribute to both the necessity and grace of brokenness. "The sun rose above him as he passed Peniel, and he was limping because of his hip. Therefore to this day the Israelites do not eat the tendon attached to the socket of the hip, because the socket of

Jacob's hip was touched near the tendon" (32:31–32).

It would have been hilarious to see Jacob walking into camp the next day with his hair disheveled, his clothes torn, his face dirty, and his lip split. Rachel blurts out, "Jacob, what in the world happened to you?" He grins and replies, "I just got blessed." Perhaps she rejoined, "Looks to me like you just got broken." And Jacob, nodding in agreement, might truly have said, "Same thing!" The New Testament contains this gem. "By faith Jacob, when he was dying, blessed each of Joseph's sons, and worshiped as he leaned on the top of his staff" (Heb. 11:21). Why was he leaning on his staff? Because he'd been crippled at Jabbok. Everywhere he went, he went with a crutch, because God had broken him. And all of his life he worshiped leaning. Jacob had learned that it is better for us to limp through life leaning on God than to strut through life trusting in ourselves. Those who strut will eventually fall. But those whom God powerfully uses and courageously infuses are those who hobble across the finish line broken but invincible in God's strength, humbled but unstoppable in God's power. Such is not just the necessity, but the beauty of brokenness.

So it was with me that afternoon thirty years ago at Medical City Dallas Hospital. My silly pride broken by facing my utter helplessness, I stood by Alice's side in the operating room and watched the doctor lift my little one-pound-twelve-ounce daughter from womb to world. Tears streamed from my eyes and absolutely drenched my surgical mask as I watched a skilled medical team insert a central line into a tiny artery and rush Bonnie to the Neonatal Intensive Care Unit, where they worked around the clock to bring that child back from the brink of death numerous times. Alice made a swift recovery, but Bonnie was not only a tiny baby; she was a very sick baby as well. Every passing day was a new river-wrestling experience for Alice and me as God broke our pride and prostrated us every morning with desperate prayer to Him for Bonnie's life with Dr. Mitch Voelker, Bonnie's neonatal doc. We also visited Bonnie as a family twice a day, in utter weakness and helplessness, holding older siblings Julie (5) and Liz (3) up to the NICU windows so they could see their little sis all hooked up in the incubator. I was further humbled and blessed as our church rallied around us, cooking meals and doing our laundry (and learning the brand and condition of our underwear and socks!). Daily broken. Daily humbled. Daily blessed. Every day for ten weeks. When Bonnie reached the whopping weight of four pounds, they let us bring our little girl home on her actual due date, two days before Christmas. She's an all-grown-up Cinderella story now, a veritable miracle of God and for years a committed foreign missionary in a very difficult field. And nobody knows better than I that God alone did that. Nobody knows better than I that God (not I) alone gets all the glory for it too (and everything else), all the time. And for the last thirty years of ministry (which began just months after Bonnie came home), I've gratefully experienced the truth of John Eldredge's words. "True strength does not come out of bravado. Until we are broken, our life will be self-centered, self-reliant; our strength will be our own. So long as you think you are really something in and of yourself, what will you need God for? I don't trust a man who hasn't suffered; I don't let a man get close to me who hasn't faced his wound."[7] David was a broken man who faced his wound and killed a giant. Jacob was a broken man who faced his wound and wrestled with God. Both were hurt deeply by God as a prelude to being used greatly by God as eminently courageous servants of God. That's the way to brave. And that's the beauty of brokenness.

Chapter 6

THE BEAUTIFUL BROKEN

My God, I have never thanked Thee for my thorns. I have thanked
Thee a thousand times for my roses, but not once for my thorns. I have
been looking forward to a world where I shall get compensation for my
cross: but I have never thought of my cross as itself a present glory.
Teach me the glory of my cross: teach me the value of my thorn.
Shew me that I have climbed to Thee by the path of pain. Shew me
that my tears have made my rainbow. —GEORGE MATHESON

But he said to me, "My grace is sufficient for you, for my power is made
perfect in weakness." Therefore I will boast all the more gladly about my
weaknesses, so that Christ's power may rest on me. That is why, for Christ's
sake, I delight in weaknesses, in insults, in hardships, in persecutions, in
difficulties. For when I am weak, then I am strong. —2 CORINTHIANS 12:9–10

My title for this chapter may strike you as a classic oxymoron if
you don't understand how I'm using the word "broken." So please
allow me to explain! I live in Texas, where ranchers regularly
"break" wild, fiercely strong-willed horses. This does not mean
those ranchers hurt, wound, or punish their (often *very* valuable)
mares and stallions. On the contrary, it means that they place their
animals in circumstances that subdue their defiant wills and thus
focus their immense power and strength on great achievement.
If you've ever seen a highly trained Texas cutting horse in action,
you've seen a magnificent creature whose initial "breaking" was
the first step to ultimate flourishing.

David's Cinderella-story upbringing as the youngest of six sons was the "circumstance" that God planned in his life to "break" David's pride early in favor of a humble desire that God get all glory. So it is for us all. Our "breaking" experiences are the result of living in a broken world with people broken with us by sin (our own and others') and circumstances beyond our control.

God only used Moses when broken of his temper, Paul when broken of his arrogance, Peter when broken of his independence, and Jacob when broken of his self-sufficiency.

Without God's higher perspective, I naturally hate these circumstances because they are generally painful, usually unfair, and always highly aggravating. In this way, I am so different from God, and probably so are you. He can make broken things powerfully useful in ways that I'm normally oblivious to until it actually happens. God only used Moses when broken of his temper, Paul when broken of his arrogance, Peter when broken of his independence, and Jacob when broken of his self-sufficiency. Vance Havner confirms God's penchant for the beautiful broken. "God uses broken things. Broken soil to produce a crop, broken clouds to give rain, broken grain to give bread, broken bread to give strength. It is the broken alabaster box that gives forth perfume."[1] And it was the brokenness that God allowed in David's life that gave him poor-in-spirit confidence that, even though it was Goliath in front of him, it was God behind him. This is our compelling hope too—that the courageous fragrance of poor-in-spirit lives broken and poured out will produce three beautiful results in our lives: our hearts will be rehabilitated, our newfound authenticity will empower us, and our humble confidence will prevail.

The Beauty of a Rehabilitated Heart

In Florence's Academia Museum, you can see four partially finished sculptures by Michelangelo Bounarotti collectively known as the *Captives*. These were figures the great artist intended to use on the tomb of Pope Julius, but midway through the project he decided not to use them and so ceased work on them. There is a hand protruding here, a torso of a man there, a leg, part of a head, all still sunk in stone. Theodore Roder writes of the *Captives*, "When I looked at those partial figures, they stirred up in me a deep longing to be completed—an ache to be set free from that which distorts and disguises, imprisons and inhibits my humanness, my wholeness. But as with those statues, I cannot liberate myself. For that I need the hand of another."[2]

When I saw the *Captives* statues a couple of years ago, I had the same gut-level reaction as Roder. I long for freedom, but freedom only comes from having my stony heart broken and rehabbed by God. What is the "heart" in Scripture? John Eldredge explains the "heart" this way: "The Bible sees the heart as the source of all creativity, courage, and conviction. It is the source of our faith, our hope, and of course, our love. It is the 'wellspring of life' within us (Prov. 4:23), the very essence of our existence, the center of our being, the fount of our life."[3] Sin is a great enemy of our hearts, though. As broken people living in a broken world, our selfishness and pride and lust and hate and greed and bitterness and rage and violence and deceit clog our spiritual arteries. Even as born-again followers of Jesus, we can struggle with spiritual arteriosclerosis. We can grow hard-hearted as if spiritually encased in stone. In a sense, all of our hearts are captive until God sets us free.

But good news: that's exactly what He promised He'd do! "I

will give you a new heart and put a new spirit in you; I will remove
from you your heart of stone and give you a heart of flesh. And I
will put my Spirit in you and move you to follow my decrees and
be careful to keep my laws" (Ezek. 36:26–27). Heart rehab. That's
what the gospel promises. "A new heart." The "hand of another,"
the Lord Jesus Christ, will chisel off our hearts of stone and help
us become all God intended us to be. He wants to set us free from
sins that distort and inhibit us. That's where brokenness comes in.
God uses pain to chisel the stone and rehab our hearts.

The problem is, rehabbing our hearts is a painful process that
we often, understandably, resist to our heart-health's detriment.
As Alan Nelson says,

> What happens when we resist the pruning process, when our
> difficult circumstances do not result in a yielding of our soul?
> I call this being broken in the wrong place. People who resist
> the elements that seek to tenderize their spirits usually end
> up as the walking wounded. They are all around us in our of-
> fices, homes, schools, and even churches. Perhaps the most
> common walking wounded is the person who is sour and
> bitter, who has an underground river of anger ready to burst
> through the surface like a geyser. Some carry the agonizing
> hurt inflicted by a parent, spouse, pastor, or boss. Others
> blame God directly for the pain of their broken dreams and
> lack of fulfillment.[4]

Here's the challenge that lies before all who seek the way of
brave. It passes through brokenness, and each of us as individual
pilgrims has the choice to be the broken beautiful or to be the
broken bitterful. C. S. Lewis trenchantly describes the stakes of
that choice. "Every time you make a choice you are turning the

central part of you, the part of you that chooses, into something a little different from what it was before. And taking your life as a whole, with all your innumerable choices, all your life long you are slowly turning this central thing either into a heavenly creature or into a hellish creature; either into a creature that is in harmony with God, and with other creatures, and with itself, or else into one that is in a state of war and hatred with God, and with its fellow-creatures, and with itself."[5] When David was broken early in his life, he established the pattern of turning, not away from God in bitter hatred, but toward God in humble trust. One clue to this reality is found in God's words about David in the New Testament. "After removing Saul, he made David their king. God testified concerning him: 'I have found David son of Jesse, a man after my own heart; he will do everything I want him to do'" (Acts 13:22–23). God knew David was a man after His own heart because brokenness had humbled his pride. God knew David was a man after His own heart because brokenness had made him obedient. That's the new heart that the gospel promises. Having broken us, He wants to make us beautiful.

In 1464, the City Council of Florence commissioned a sculptor to carve a giant statue of a biblical character to stand in front of city hall. Agostino di Duccio went to the quarry and marked off a nineteen-foot slab to be cut from the white marble. However, when the block was removed, it fell, leaving a deep fracture down one side. The sculptor declared the stone useless and demanded another, but the council refused. Consequently, the gleaming block of marble lay on its side for thirty-eight years. Then, in 1501, the council asked Michelangelo if he would complete the project. He locked himself inside his workshop to chisel the stone for three years. When the work was finished, it took forty-nine men five days to bring it to city hall. For six hundred years, people have flocked from around the world to see Michelangelo's fourteen-foot sculpture we know today simply as *David*. Unlike with the *Captives*, the great artist had completed his chiseling and totally freed his masterpiece from stone, just like God had done thirteen centuries before in rehabbing the flesh-and-blood David's heart.[6]

The Beauty of an Authentic Soul

One of the scariest places to live one's life is behind a mask. All is well if the mask stays in place. But just let it slip ever so slightly, and the terror of "unmasking" stalks our soul. Will people discover that I'm not as confident, omni-talented, and impervious to pressure as the "persona" I've so assiduously constructed would lead them to believe? Once more, John Eldredge writes, "We are hiding, every last one of us. Well aware that we, too, are not what we were meant to be, desperately afraid of exposure, terrified of being seen for what we are and are not, we have run off into the bushes. We hide in our office, at the gym, behind the newspaper and mostly behind our personality. Most of what you encounter when you meet a man is a façade, an elaborate fig leaf, a brilliant disguise."[7] So Walter Anderson raises a penetrating question: "Hundreds of times I have looked into the eyes of a successful person and asked, 'When it is dark and you are alone, do you ever say to yourself, What will I do when they find out I'm me?'"[8] That's the fundamental fearfulness all who nervously manage in-authentic souls, and I admit that some form of that question pops into my own mind every time I stand to teach the Scriptures to a group of people. "What will I do when they find out I'm me?" Yep. Whether I like it or not, that question still occasionally per-colates at the subconscious level in my pastor brain! But I suspect I am not alone in my tendency to hide. Since the infamous first fig leaf, covering up our true selves and struggles and pain is the default mode of the human race.

I got my first fig leaf in the fourth grade. Our family had moved from West Virginia to a very small town in Alabama just in time for me to start a new school, where I soon felt ostra-

Since the infamous first fig leaf, covering up our true selves and struggles and pain is the default mode of the human race.

cized and, as a result, worthless. For months. And then spring came, along with outside recesses and slow-pitch softball. On that day the cool kids were choosing sides to play, and naturally I got chosen last and made to wait till last to hit. But when I made it up to bat, a life-changing event occurred. Much to my own amazement, and especially to the surprise of the other kids, I smashed the first pitch I got right out of the place. It went so far, nobody even moved to get it. They just all watched me round the bases with astonishment and gaping mouths. Their response was not lost on me. I *loved* it! I found life in it. I wanted more of it. A lot more of it!

So I began right there and then to construct my façade of omni-competence, my elaborate fig leaf of athletic prowess, my brilliant disguise of competitive success. Game on! I spent the next twenty years desperately driven to protect my soul from the pain of rejection by graduating high school in the top five as a multi-sport letterman (all-district on my Texas football team) who was also president of the National Honor Society who got a football scholarship to college. No more fourth grade misery for me! I kept the pedal to the metal in college, making the dean's list and graduating with high honors. I went ahead and did basically the same thing through two postgraduate degrees. No more getting chosen last for the team on the playground, just relentless running and careful façade-building for this son of an Irish immigrant. But all the time

I wondered, "What will I do when they find out I'm me?!" Then I read Brennan Manning and gratefully marveled to know that I was not alone, that my story was his story, too. "When I was eight, the imposter, or false self, was born as a defense against pain. The impostor within whispered, 'Brennan, don't ever be your real self anymore because nobody likes you as you are. Invent a new self that everybody will admire and nobody will know.' So I became a good boy—polite, well-mannered, unobtrusive, and deferential. . . . and was stalked every waking moment by the terror of abandonment and the sense that nobody was there for me."[9]

All these years later, I'm convinced that God let Brennan and me (and perhaps you, too?) go on this wild goose chase because He knew it's the only way I'd learn that the courage we create with our imposter selves is a chimera! There is no game you can win, no award you can receive, no achievement you can attain, no acclaim you can command that permanently grants you reprieve from the question, "What will I do when they find out I'm me?" The only thing that can grant such a reprieve is brokenness, which leads to vulnerability, which leads to beauty.

> **The courage we create with our imposter selves is a chimera! The only thing that can grant a reprieve from the question "What will I do when they find out I'm me?" is brokenness, which leads to vulnerability, which leads to beauty.**

In a famous TED Talk with over thirty million views to date, Brené Brown spoke these words of wisdom: "whole-hearted people . . . are willing to let go of who they thought they should be in order to be who they were. . . . They fully embraced vulnerability. They believed that what made them vulnerable made them beautiful. This is what I

have found: To let ourselves be seen, deeply seen, vulnerably seen
. . . is to love with our whole hearts."[10] Sometimes God knows
that it's too hard for us to do alone what needs to be done. Like
Michaelangelo's *Captives*, we need the help of another to free us,
and God does that through breaking us. This painful process of
exposing our weakness and need removes the very basis of our
imposter's fear—the fear of being exposed. And so as firefight-
ers neutralize racing wildfires by preemptive, controlled burning,
so God neutralizes the paralyzing fear of exposure by preemptive
exposure. He lovingly breaks us by poking holes in our façade,
plucking our elaborate fig leaves, and revealing our brilliant disguises. With nothing left to be exposed, we also have nothing left
to fear. So writes Ann Voskamp. "When you know you're never
alone in the fear, you lose the fear of the fear. Not being afraid of
even being afraid—may be the bravest way of all."[11]

That's exactly what happened to Ronnie Stanley back in 1961.
It had been a tough year for this senior quarterback for the Baylor
Bears. He'd lost his starting job to a sophomore underclassman.
Ignored by the head coach and banished to the bench, he still
hoped for one more chance. It came in the last minute of the last
game of Stanley's football career. The setting was the 1961 Gotham
Bowl, an ill-fated promotional attempt in the early 60s to create the
Rose Bowl of the east. Played in the creaking old Polo Grounds in
New York City, "The Gotham" that year featured unbeaten Utah
State against underdog Baylor on a frigid December afternoon.
The crowd? A sparse few hundred. The weather? Freezing and
bleak. The music? The New York City Department of Sanitation
Band. They proudly provided half-time entertainment clad in their
occupational "uniforms"—dingy work overalls. The competition?
A yawner. Baylor racked up a 24–3 lead by game's end.

Ronnie Stanley's opportunity for redemption came in the

God neutralizes the paralyzing fear of exposure by preemptive exposure. He lovingly breaks us by poking holes in our façade, plucking our elaborate fig leaves, and revealing our brilliant disguises.

final seconds of this forgettable game. The coach put him in for the last play, albeit at great disadvantage. His arm was cold, but he had instructions to throw deep. As he faded back to pass, an opponent hammered him, breaking Stanley's leg just as he released the football. His "wounded duck" pass was intercepted and returned for hapless Utah's only touchdown.

My heart goes out to Ronnie Stanley. As an old high-school quarterback, I've thrown my share of fluttering interceptions and endured my share of broken bones. It's a sickening feeling to descend so precipitously from the glory status you'd dreamed to the "goat" status you'd dreaded. But in any disappointment contest, I readily surrender to Stanley.

He spent that night alone in a New York hospital room while his teammates celebrated their win at the Peppermint Lounge, a famous Manhattan nightspot. Between pain pills, embarrassing memory flashes of his pitiful pass attempt and the humiliating season that preceded it tortured Ronnie Stanley. Here he was, a former star ignominiously bereft of his starter status, shunned by the coach, playing his last down of football on a dismal day in a dilapidated stadium before a few belligerent fans and a garbage department band. How's that for going out with a bang? He'd entered a meaningless game for a meaningless play and a meaningless injury with the result that his suddenly terminated football career seemed a meaningless waste. Now he would spend Christmas in a cast, away from home, all alone, and literally, broken.

But Ronnie's turned out to be a beautiful broken. Ronnie

Stanley wrote these words to a Dallas sportswriter twenty years after his humiliating demise in the Gotham Bowl:

> That fractured tibia was one of the best things that ever happened to me. Placing a cast on our leg is not supposed to help your eyesight, but my vision cleared remarkably with a cast, some pain and some time . . .While recovering from the broken leg, my eyesight now saw a wonderful mother and dad and sisters. It also helped me see the real worth of the girl I was dating. You know, when you engage in football for eight to nine years in a row, it's like heroin. It's difficult to separate yourself from it. You are fearful that there won't be any "me" left, after he athlete has been removed. The broken leg served as a cleavage plane and I broke free, much to my benefit.
>
> I married that girl and I still love her. She's gotten more attractive to me. I have three fine sons and a beautiful daughter . . . I guess we all should be more grateful and thankful for everything in our lives, yes, for the bad, also. Sometimes bad is not bad, it's good. I've been here now since 1970 and my leg carries me for a three mile jog every other day along a sandy road in Hopkins County and I sometimes think of the Polo Grounds, the band with the funny uniforms and the trip I missed to the Peppermint Lounge.[12]

That letter was written on stationary from the Sulphur Springs Medical-Surgical Clinic and signed: "Ronald T. Stanley, M.D." For this broken quarterback, the "bad" was meant for "good" (remember, however, that sometimes bad is still bad, even though God promises to bring good from it), and he became a faithful husband, a loving father, and a beloved physician with a rehabbed heart and an authentic soul . . . what a beautiful thing.

The Beauty of Quiet Courage

The quiet courage that Ronnie Stanley displayed in moving past his humiliation at the Gotham Bowl is also beautiful. It took gumption for him to overcome, not just the pain of a broken leg, but the end of his dream of becoming a player in the National Football League. The Gotham Bowl had been a *breaking* experience for him, yet Jesus says it was also a *blessed* experience for him. "Blessed are the poor in spirit, for theirs is the kingdom of heaven" (Matt. 5:3).

Power and position in any kingdom, it would seem, comes as a reward for a job well done, a task successfully finished, a résumé well-burnished with rich accolades. Just watching TV ads teaches this, right? In our worldly kingdom, "blessed are those who fly to luxury vacation spots on tropical islands and lie in chaise lounge chairs, the only people on an enormous white beach, for they shall be satisfied. Blessed are those who have the latest smartphone, for they shall gaze on a screen swirling with color and shall get all the information they need just when they need it, and they shall be satisfied. Blessed are those who have outstanding kids. Verily I say to you, highly blessed are those who have a golden Labrador retriever bounding along on that slow-motion-videoed day of playing with the kids in the park, for they shall be the envy of real families everywhere, and they shall be satisfied."[13]

But no. Jesus says otherwise. The very success and wealth and self-confidence that the world defines as blessing, He says can be a huge spiritual distraction. Jesus said, "How hard it is for the rich to enter the kingdom of God!" (Mark 10:23). Those who are rich may not apprehend their true spiritual powerlessness until it's too late because their money may make them think they can manage their lives apart from God. The great challenge here is to recognize that poverty of spirit is a continuing reality, not a fixable short-term problem. We are desperate and dependent on God, and we're blessed in our desperation because entrance into Christ's kingdom is counterintuitive.

Hence the gift to faithful Christ followers of living a joyful and fruitful life in God's kingdom comes as a reward for *stopping* already with the fig leaves and façades to live gratefully as those who God made them to be. God did not make Ronnie to be a pro quarterback. God did make Ronnie to be a beloved physician. But it took a broken tibia to push the eventual Dr. Stanley in the right direction.

Blessed then are those with heart-rehabbed, authentic, poor-in-spirit souls! They, like all of us, whether we recognize it or not, have come to the end of their ropes. It's just that they are no longer too proud to admit it. Their refusal to live in denial gives them the power of authenticity and puts the kingdom squarely in their grasp. As Clarence Jordan wrote, "God does not force his kingdom upon anybody but gladly gives it to all who know they're losers without him and humbly seek his help."[14]

God has a special purpose for all of His children's lives. The way He deals with you in your life is not a duplicate of His dealing with anybody else, anywhere else. That does not mean God is unfair. It means that He has a different purpose for and glory in and about each life.

Those are the ones who, in coming to the end of their fig-leaf façades, have also come to embrace the true, authentic selves God made them to be. Young David had a lot of stone chiseled away from his soul by the breaking experiences in his life. That painful process was a great blessing, though, because when the stone façade crumbled, what remained behind fairly melted David's heart with its beauty. "For you created my inmost being; you knit me together in my mother's womb. I praise you because I am fearfully and wonderfully made; your works are wonderful, I know that full well" (Ps. 139:13–14). As David was, you and I are—one-of-a kind people! God made twenty-five thousand varieties of orchids, but He made billions of varieties of people—each one as a heavenly original.

But also as David was, you and I are—one-of-a-kind persons handcrafted for a divine purpose. "Your eyes saw my unformed body; all the days ordained for me were written in your book before one of them came to be" (v. 16). God has a special purpose for all of His children's lives. The way He deals with you in your life is not a duplicate of His dealing with anybody else, anywhere else. Some people have a relatively smooth life; others suffer greatly. Some people seem to get all the breaks; others encounter one heartache after another. That does not mean God is unfair. It means that He has a different purpose for and glory in and about each life. Our response to God's unique purpose and plan for each of us should be to make a declaration of independence from the expectations of the world and start performing for an audience of one—the Lord Himself. This is true maturity: the ability to do what God has called and gifted me to do and not care what people think!

This also is the way to brave. Those who are poor in spirit through being broken have lost the fear of exposure by embracing the person God made them to be. The power of authenticity flows from losing the fear of the fear. Gordon MacDonald points out how this happened in Moses's life.

Moses encountered failure when he impulsively killed an Egyptian. He paid for his mistake over a 40 year stretch in the desert . . . the man who emerges at the other end of the 40 years is different. Still a bit defiant at times? Sure. But nevertheless, he's now a listener. He can stand his ground in tough moments. He hungers for God's glory, demonstrates obedience (usually), and seems to truly grasp God's purposes for his people. The prefailure Moses would never have had the right stuff to lead those people through the wilderness. I wonder if Moses would ever have learned to do things God's way if it had not been for his earlier failure and its consequences?[15]

No need to wonder; the answer based on unbroken human nature is a resounding no! It was God's breaking of Moses during those forty years that humbled his heart and put him on the way to brave. As Ann Voskamp stated, "Not being afraid of even being afraid—may be the bravest way of all."[16]

Knowing that failures help us learn to do things God's way means that we never have to fear being afraid in the first place. Moses learned that, and we can as well. So let's embrace being the beautiful broken.

GOD TESTS US

1 SAMUEL 17:33–37

Saul replied, "You are not able to go out against this Philistine and fight him; you are only a young man, and he has been a warrior from his youth." But David said to Saul, "Your servant has been keeping his father's sheep. When a lion or a bear came and carried off a sheep from the flock, I went after it, struck it and rescued the sheep from its mouth. When it turned on me, I seized it by its hair, struck it and killed it. Your servant has killed both the lion and the bear; this uncircumcised Philistine will be like one of them, because he has defied the armies of the living God. The LORD who rescued me from the paw of the lion and the paw of the bear will rescue me from the hand of this Philistine."

ONLY A TESTED FAITH is a courageous faith. David's courage in volunteering to fight the giant was not a leap of bravado, but a considered decision.

God had stair-stepped David's faith to Goliath heights through the testing of lion and bear. Each new victory supplemented David's confidence-quotient to such a degree that when the ultimate test menaced, David's faith answered.

Knowing that his was a tested and proven faith made David brave. And it will make us and our families brave too if we do not resist, but welcome God's testing of our faith as well. As James writes, "Consider it pure joy, my brothers and sisters, whenever you face trials of many kinds, because you know that the testing of your faith produces perseverance. Let perseverance finish its work so that you may be mature and complete, not lacking anything" (1:2–4). Indeed, let it finish its work.

Chapter 7

LIONS AND TIGERS AND BEARS (AND GIANTS), OH MY!

A great part of courage is the courage of having done the thing before.
—RALPH WALDO EMERSON

A day may come when the courage of men fails, when we forsake our friends and break all bonds of fellowship, but it is not this day. An hour of wolves and shattered shields, when the age of men comes crashing down, but it is not this day. This day we fight! By all that you hold dear on this good Earth, I bid you stand, Men of the West! —ARAGORN IN *LORD OF THE RINGS: THE RETURN OF THE KING*

I have to think it was a royal pain for David to shepherd sheep in lion and bear country. Not only did these predators pose a constant threat to his sheep, they posed a constant threat to David's very life. Their presence meant that watching over the sheep was a matter of life and death. No half-asleep sidelong glances while sipping piña coladas and catching up on the *Jerusalem Post* sports page. David had to be fixated on a threat that he dreaded ever materializing. Who wants to wage single combat in the dead (pun intended) of night with lions and bears, oh my (sorry, no tigers in Israel), especially when they're armed with powerful agility and razor claws and your only weapon is a string and a rock? Manifestly an undesirable situation.

Yet, it came to David, again and again, with unmitigated constancy and increasing ferocity. "Your servant has been keeping his father's sheep. When a lion or a bear came and carried off a sheep from the flock, I went after it, struck it and rescued the sheep from its mouth. When it turned on me, I seized it by its hair, struck it and killed it" (1 Sam. 17:34–35). When I was sixteen, I liked to play basketball and watch movies. But David's adolescence was spent matching brawn and wits with wild animals that wanted to kill him and eat his sheep. I had a far tamer time of it for sure, but just as certain is that the untamed tests of David's youth fitted him far more than me for extraordinary courage that would show up on a distant day in a deep valley against a fearsome giant.

God had tested David with lions and bears, not to harm him physically or incapacitate him spiritually, but to strengthen his faith and fortify his confidence. Only shepherds who've killed lions and bears even think of stepping into the ring with giants.

Economist Nassim Taleb "coined the phrase 'anti-fragile' to encapsulate a quality of resilience and security that can be built into economic systems so they can withstand unforeseeable disruptive events."[1] The way to brave lies through times of testing and trials that make us "anti-fragile." David's courage against Goliath was a product of his testing by the lion and the bear. "Your servant has killed both the lion and the bear; this uncircumcised Philistine will be like one of them, because he has defied the armies of the living

God. The LORD who rescued me from the paw of the lion and the paw of the bear will rescue me from the hand of this Philistine" (1 Sam. 17:36–37).

God had tested David with lions and bears, not to harm him physically or incapacitate him spiritually, but to strengthen his faith and fortify his confidence. Only shepherds who've killed lions and bears even think of stepping into the ring with giants. Each new victory supplemented David's confidence-quotient to such a degree that when the ultimate test menaced, David's faith answered. In this way God shaped a David faith for a Goliath world. And in this way God will shape our faith as well. It's just how He does it. As James writes, "Consider it pure joy, my brothers and sisters, whenever you face trials of many kinds, because you know that the testing of your faith produces perseverance. Let perseverance finish its work so that you may be mature and complete, not lacking anything" (James 1:2–4). Testing, then, is an essential experience on our way to brave because God uses it to mature and complete our faith by *broadening*, *deepening*, and *focusing* our faith.

Testing Broadens Faith

One of my heroes growing up was the late great Charles Schultz's cartoon creation Charlie Brown. For Charlie Brown, nothing in life ever went just right. He couldn't get the Little Red-Haired Girl's attention. Lucy always pulled the football away when he tried to kick it. His own dog Snoopy always outsmarted him. And his ball team never won (ever). In one of my favorite strips, even the simple pleasure of flying a kite eluded Charlie Brown when he got his caught in a tree. So when he hears his friend Peppermint Patty say, "I need to talk to someone who knows what it's like to feel like a fool . . . someone who knows what it's like to be humiliated . . . someone who's been disgraced, beaten and degraded . . . someone who's been there," Charlie Brown just throws up his arms as if to say, "I'm your man." I've been your man too, Peppermint Patty.

My natural response when trials come my way is the same as a guy who was waiting at a crowded New York subway stop at the front of the line. The train stopped, and the doors opened to reveal a very pale-looking man standing there. This man had been fighting motion sickness, but just as the door opened he lost the battle. He upchucked all over the guy in line, after which the doors closed and the train pulled out. The guy turned to the crowd, threw his hands in the air and cried, "Why me?!" That is the operative question in every human heart when trials come. James answers that question concisely. "Consider it pure joy, my brothers and sisters, whenever you face trials of many kinds, because you know that the testing of your faith produces perseverance" (James 1:2–3).

But what happens when the joy and contentment that James speaks about doesn't happen immediately in our trials? Sometimes the angst and lament we feel as we cry out "Why me?!" lingers for a while. Sometimes that pain sticks around, despite our knowledge that God is in control and trials are for a purpose. Oftentimes the weight of heartache and sorrow over a trial far outweigh the knowledge that when my faith is tested I'm learning perseverance. It's okay to cry "Why me?!" Jesus identifies with us in our pain and trials. We should grieve the pain of this fallen world, but we can also embrace God's promises in faith and trust in His sovereignty. It's not either/or, but it is both/and.

Something that I have found helpful in painful times is to recognize that it's not just you and me that have our faith tested. It's *everyone*. Trials are inevitable for all: "*whenever* [not if] you face trials of many kinds." M. Scott Peck acknowledges that fact in the first line of his old bestseller *The Road Less Travelled*: "Life is difficult." Yes, life is difficult, but James assures us that for us as believers, it's difficult *for a purpose*. We may not feel the truth of that statement in the moment, but God sends trials to broaden our faith in Him, to deepen our dependence on Him, to remind us that He is God.

Following the Winter Olympic Games a few years ago, Ameritrade aired an ad that I still love. It began by showing the US Olympic snowboarder Louie Vito standing hand-on-heart on the gold medal podium while the American National Anthem played. Then the ad takes us backwards on the timeline of Vito's life. We see a clip of him as a young man performing advanced tricks (and falling hard) with the assistance of a long metal railing. The next clip shows the 2002 Louie as a teenager "catching air" on the slopes (and wiping out often). In other clips he's a child practicing flips on a trampoline, unwrapping a snowboard on Christmas morning, and blowing out two candles on his birthday cake. The last scene shows Vito, who looks barely old enough to stand, snowboarding down a sloping front yard and then getting scooped up by an adult as these words appear on the screen: "Behind every big moment, there are lots of small ones." That's the encouragement that James offers to us on the way to brave. Lots of small moments ("trials of many kinds") fit us out to succeed in the big moments when a mature and complete faith is so essential for success.

That's the very reason the apostle Peter has such a glowing attitude toward trials. "In all this you greatly rejoice, though now for a little while you may have had to suffer grief in all kinds of trials. These have come so that the proven genuineness of your faith— of greater worth than gold, which perishes even though refined by fire—may result in praise, glory and honor when Jesus Christ is revealed" (1 Peter 1:6–7). Peter probably wrote these words from Rome shortly before he was put to death under the brutal persecution of Emperor Nero in the mid-60s AD. A reign of terror had begun in the capital city when Christians were falsely blamed by him for a major fire in Rome. The brutality that followed was ruthless. It is to such horrors that Peter refers as suffering grief "in all kinds of trials . . . so that the proven genuineness of your faith—of greater worth than gold, which perishes even though refined by fire—may result in praise, glory and honor when Jesus Christ is revealed." He holds that God does not allow his people to go through "all kinds of trials" (literally, "multicolored") so that their faith fails, but rather so that their faith is refined. Hardships do not divert them *from* Christ; trials drive them *to* Christ so that their faith becomes broader and stronger and more beautiful for His glory.

A young man wanted to be a peach grower and invested everything he had in an orchard. Finally it blossomed, but a frost came and killed his peach crop. He told his pastor, "I'm done with God. Do you think I want to worship a God who cares for me so little that He will let a frost kill all of my peaches?" The old minister was silent for a few moments, then kindly said, "God loves you more than your peaches. He knows that while peaches do better without frost, it is impossible to grow the best men without frost. His object is to grow men, not peaches."[2]

Here's what a Christian knows that makes him have a peculiar response to trials: "God isn't at work producing the circumstances *you* want. God is at work in bad circumstances to produce the *you* He wants."[3] That's good with me because the me my Living Savior wants is way better than any me I could ever hope to be. As the great George Whitefield wrote, "I have put my soul, as a blank, into the hands of Jesus Christ my Redeemer, and desired him to write upon it what he pleases. I know it will be his own image."[4]

In 1982, two Russian cosmonauts touched down after 211 days in the space station Salyut 7. At zero gravity, their muscles had atrophied due to complete lack of resistance. For a week they were unable to walk, and "after 30 days, they were still undergoing therapy for atrophied muscles and weakened hearts. . . . To counteract this, the Soviets. . . . invented the 'penguin suit,' a running suit laced with elastic bands" that "resisted every move the cosmonauts made, forcing them to exert extra strength." In 1987, another "Soviet cosmonaut returned to the earth after 326 days in orbit," but unlike those before him, this guy was in top shape the moment he got home. The penguin suit had helped the cosmonaut stay strong by adding resistance to his movements.[5] Sounds like *beneficial* trials to me!

God strengthens our character qualities by resisting them with their opposites. We learn true peace in the midst of chaos. We learn to love by being around unlovely people. We learn true joy in the midst of tragedy, patience in the midst of waiting, and kindness in the face of cruelty.

So my friends, get ready for trials on the way to brave. And not just one. A steady stream. A constant exercise. A cascade of lions and tigers and bears and giants (oh my!) is God's gift (albeit sometimes you might rather reject the gift because it causes too much pain) to broaden your faith from a narrow band of coverage to complete coverage of what may come. Trials mature your faith so that it can courageously interact with anything this world can throw at you! Think of it this way: God strengthens our character qualities by resisting them with their opposites. We learn true peace in the midst of chaos. We learn to love by being around unlovely people. We learn true joy in the midst of tragedy, patience in the midst of waiting, and kindness in the face of cruelty. As Ben Jonson says: "He knows not his own strength that hath not met adversity. Heaven prepares good men with crosses."[6] So my friends, gladly don the penguin suit! It will keep you strong. Gladly welcome trials! They will broaden and complete your faith.

Testing Deepens Faith

James continues to explain the lions and tigers and bears that God sends into our lives. "If any of you lacks wisdom, you should ask God, who gives generously to all without finding fault, and it will be given to you. But when you ask, you must believe and not doubt, because the one who doubts is like a wave of the sea, blown and tossed by the wind. That person should not expect to receive anything from the Lord. Such a person is double-minded and unstable in all they do" (James 1:5–8).

Not only does God send trials to broaden our faith, but to deepen it as well. Our faith grows deeper as we acquire wisdom— the ability to see life from God's point of view. We can only gain such wisdom by getting close to God: "The fear of the LORD is the beginning of wisdom, and the knowledge of the Holy One is understanding" (Prov. 9:10).

So how do we get close to God? You guessed it! Trials. Trials rattle us out of complacency and cause us to truly seek and depend on Him. As J. I. Packer observed,

When we walk along a clear road feeling fine, and someone takes our arm to help us, likely we would impatiently shake him off; but when we are caught in rough country in the dark, with a storm brewing and our strength spent, and someone takes our arm to help us, we would thankfully lean on him. And God wants us to feel that our way through life is rough and perplexing, so that we may learn to lean on him thankfully. Therefore he takes steps to drive us out of self-confidence to trust in himself, to—in the classic scriptural phrase for the secret of the godly man's life—"wait on the Lord."[7]

This is why God allows troubles and perplexities of one sort and another into our lives. He wants us to learn how to hold on to Him. The reason the Bible spends so much time reiterating that God is a strong rock, a firm defense, and a sure refuge for the weak is that alone, we are weak, both mentally and morally, and dare not trust ourselves to find or follow the right road by our own devices. We desperately need His guidance. We deeply long for His wisdom. The good news is that when we're confused and hurting and need the Lord, He promises to give us needed perspective, essential wisdom—without making us feel stupid or foolish, as He did in answer to this soldier's Civil War prayer.

I asked God for strength that I might achieve. I was made weak that I might learn humbly to obey. I asked God for health that I might do greater things. I was given infirmity that I might do better things. I asked for riches that I might be happy. I was given poverty that I might be wise. I asked for power that I might have the praise of men. I was given weakness that I might feel the need of God. I asked for all things that I might enjoy life. I was given life that I might enjoy all things. I got nothing that I asked for—but everything I had hoped for. Almost despite myself, my unspoken prayers were answered. I am among all men most richly blessed.[8]

But notice from James the requirement for receiving faith-deepening wisdom: asking without doubting. The word "doubt" (*diakrino*) literally means "a divided calling or judgment." What is it, especially in times of trouble, that James says we have to make up our mind about? In context, the goodness of God about whom James has just asserted "He gives to all men generously and without reproach." If that's true, then God is a good, loving God who wants what's best for us. To doubt the goodness of God in times of trial while seeking God's help, James says, is to be a double-minded person, literally a "two-souled" man. Such a person has a fundamental internal conflict, approaching God for help in trials while secretly blaming and resenting God, asking for God's deliverance while cursing God's testing. How would you like it if your kid came to you and said, "Dad (or Mom), I think you're a foolish old kook. By the way, can I have the car keys for tonight?" It's likely that child will be walking. In the same way, those who come to God without having settled their opinion of Him are unstable, double-minded, and "should not expect to receive anything from the Lord." To get wisdom from your trials, then, you have to make the call about the character of God. Andrew Murray demonstrates how it's done:

> In time of trouble, say, First, He brought me here. It is by His will I am in this strait place; in that I will rest. Next, He will keep me here in his love, and give me grace in this trial to behave as his child. Then say, He will make the trial a blessing, teaching me lessons he intends me to learn, and working in

me the grace he means to bestow. And last, say, in his good time he can bring me out again. How and when, he knows. Therefore, say, I am here (1) by God's appointment, (2) in His keeping, (3) under His training, (4) for His time."[9]

Testing Focuses Faith

Finally, James gives us an eternal perspective on the tests and trials that God graciously sends into our lives. "Blessed is the one who perseveres under trial because, having stood the test, that person will receive the crown of life that the Lord has promised to those who love him" (James 1:12). Why has God sent lions and tigers and bears (and giants) into all of our lives? Two reasons: to learn God's wisdom for temporal priorities in this world, and to focus our faith on eternal priorities in the world to come.

In regard to that first reason, just days before death the late great British journalist and Christian Malcolm Muggeridge observed that trials that seem in themselves to have no purpose are, in the end, indispensable: "As an old man . . . looking back on one's life it's one of the things that strikes you most forcibly—that the only thing that's taught one anything is suffering. Not success, not happiness, not anything like that. The only thing that really teaches one what life's about . . . is suffering, affliction."[10]

If life's about a good and loving God orchestrating all the events of our lives over time into a thing of beauty, then we can relax when the chips are down. We know that whatever the problem, it's not the end of the story. That sets us free to make the best of it. Things seem to turn out best for those who make the best of the way things turn out. And making the best of things is a choice that you and I must make. It's a choice Job made. He concentrated on God's plan for him. But it's important to point out that, even while

Life's about a good and loving God orchestrating all the events of our lives over time into a thing of beauty. We know that whatever the problem, it's not the end of the story. Job remained faithful in the end, there were several chapters in the middle of Job when he grieved, lamented, mourned, and questioned God. He even said God's ways seemed cruel to him! "You have turned cruel to me; with the might of your hand you persecute me" (Job 30:21 ESV).[11] Yet, against the urging of his wife to curse God and die, he steadfastly kept his attention not on what was happening to him, but on how he could respond faithfully to it. That's job one for us as well—to respond faithfully and trust in Him no matter what trials come our way!

But, let me reiterate that while we may know this in our heads, when rubber meets the road and difficult trials come our way, getting to a place of trust and joy and contentment isn't easy or straightforward. In fact, more often than not, it proves very difficult. It's hard to trust in Him, it's easy to be bitter, and it's natural to lament and grieve. We have to come to a place of repentance and contentment through trials nevertheless, but that often is not a clean-cut or quick process—it may be filled with blood, sweat, and tears, laments and doubts, that test the genuineness of our faith and refine us.

The second reason God sends lions and tigers and bears into each of our lives is to focus our faith on eternal priorities in the world to come. During a particularly difficult season of trial and testing, the great evangelist John Wesley wrote: "I am a creature of a day, passing through life as an arrow through the air. I am a spirit, coming from God, and returning to God; just hovering over the great gulf; a few months hence I am no more seen; I drop into an unchangeable eternity! I want to know one thing—the way to heaven." God has trials to lead us all to the same faith-focusing conclusion: heaven, not earth, is our ultimate destination and therefore should be our earthly priority. Suffering is the motivation God provides us to take our eyes off temporal things so that we can see eternal realities.

The great apostle Paul's perspective on trials, like John Wesley's, is spiritually buoyant. "I count all things but loss for the excellency of the knowledge of Christ Jesus my Lord: for whom I have suffered the loss of all things, and do count them but dung, that I may win Christ" (Phil. 3:8 KJV). And like Paul and John Wesley, so Steven Curtis Chapman. Steven has five Grammys, dozens of Dove Awards, and over 11 million records sold. Early in 2017, he published a memoir, *Between Heaven and Earth*, in which he opens up about marital difficulties and the death of his five-year-old daughter. Bottom line. Those times of severe testing and heartache actually fueled his music by focusing his faith on eternal things. Steven said, "But Jesus tells us, 'In this world you will have trouble.' But then he says, 'But take heart. I have overcome the world.' He's saying there's another story being told, and if I didn't believe that I would be an extremely bitter and angry man. Maria's death underlined and solidified what I knew and believed, and made it more real. When there was nothing else to hold on to, I heard myself say, 'God, I'm going to trust you and worship you, and that's not because there's an audience watching. I'm going to bless your name whether you give or take away.'"[12]

God wants to broaden and deepen and focus your faith through trials into a thing of magnificence that He can reward for all eternity. When trials come then, understand that God is readying you for glory. So cheer up, Charlie Brown, and "consider it all joy . . . when you encounter various trials" (James 1:2 NASB)! Mark Batterson explains why.

> God is in the résumé-building business. He is always using past experiences to prepare us for future opportunities. But those God-given opportunities often come disguised as man-eating lions. And how we react when we encounter those lions will determine our destiny. We can cower in fear and run away from our greatest challenges. Or we can chase our God-ordained destiny by seizing the God-ordained opportunity.
>
> As I look back on my own life, I recognize this simple truth: The greatest opportunities were the scariest lions. Part of me has wanted to play it safe, but I've learned that taking no risks is the greatest risk of all.[13]

When the young shepherd David took his stand against Goliath in the Valley of Elah, I wonder if he breathed a prayer of thanks to God for the scary lions and bears of his not-too-distant past. They truly had been David's greatest opportunity, for in defeating them he had gained a faith broad and deep and focused enough to courageously face the giant. These trials had shaped David's faith for a Goliath world because he did not resist them as intruders but welcomed them as friends on the way to brave. It's time for us to do the same!

Chapter 8

FAITH STANDS UP

The opposite for courage is not cowardice, it is conformity.
Even a dead fish can go with the flow. —Jim Hightower

Courage is contagious. When a brave man takes a stand,
the spines of others are often stiffened. —Billy Graham

The testing of our faith is God's strategy for the deepening of our faith. Though often difficult and even painful, it is a gift from God because it moves us ahead on the way to brave. Some, however, willingly deceive themselves by rejecting out of hand "lions and tigers and bears (oh my!)" as unnecessary aggravations in what they consider our utopian postmodern age. Mark Sayers identifies the damage this mindset has done:

Millennials were privileged to be born during this post–Cold War period. Many came of age during an economic boom that lasted until the global financial crisis in 2008. This was also a period when education was permeated with the self-esteem ethos that emphasized feelings, and downplayed the possibility of disappointments and difficulties that strengthen us.

All this, coupled with the rise of social media, has given them inflated life expectations . . . because their teachers, parents, and leaders have encouraged them to live out a faulty life script.[1]

The greatest casualty of that "faulty life script" is a faith that stands up. Distrustful Christians without a tested faith cannot comprise a courageous church. We Christians in America need to regain a strong appreciation of the role of testing in the building of our faith. We need to thank God for the crucible, not vilify Him for it. It is a tested faith that runs deep, and a deep faith that stands strong in painful times and intimidating times and even dangerous times. Such deep-running, tested faith is a David faith, as exemplified on that day when the young shepherd approached an Elah Valley ringing with the painful taunts (matched by fearful sighs of the Israelite soldiers) of a blatantly intimidating and overtly dangerous giant named Goliath. David didn't back down in fear. Rather, his faith moved him to stand up. If ours is a tested faith, it will move us to stand up too.

Faith Stands Up in Painful Times

In the winter of 1984, my friend Dave Burchett and his wife Joni were not prepared for the shock of what they had anticipated would be a joyous occasion—the birth of their daughter Katie. Dave was with Joni in the delivery room when the doctor spoke the crushing words, "Your daughter has a birth defect." Little Katie had anencephaly—the failure of the brain to develop—a rare terminal condition that occurs once every twenty thousand births. David and Joni's little girl would never sit up, see, walk, or say their names. She would have constant seizures. And she would die in months.

In those days, I was a newly ordained associate pastor in David and Joni's church, and their painful family trauma was my first challenge as a spiritual shepherd trying to minister to a hurting family. And Katie's funeral was my very first funeral service

as a pastor. So you'll understand my personal struggle with this
family's pain as the question rattled constantly in my brain, "Why
would God let such a thing happen?" That's what many of you
would like to know in the big fat middle of very painful times.
Maybe your lions and tigers and bears have shown up as trage-
dies and sorrows. Your family split, your health failed, misfortune
struck your business, an accident has plunged you into chronic
physical pain, or you've borne the heartbreak of watching a loved
one die. Maybe you just want to know: How is faith possible when
hard things happen? How can my faith stand up in painful times?

Thousands of years ago, an afflicted saint named Job spent
time in the furnace of suffering. In his affliction, he persevered because of a conviction he held about God: "He knows the way that I
take; when he has tested me, I will come forth as gold" (Job 23:10).
J. R. R. Tolkien called such testings "eucatastrophes"—literally,
"good catastrophe"—because as Job declared, a powerful and
loving God uses them to make greater good come from great evil.
Hence the eucatastrophic song from Job's heart, which, having been
broken by inexplicably losing his family and health, yet sounds
forth as gold. The eucatastrophic song is a burning bush calling
a stuttering fugitive named Moses to redeem his people. It echoes
from Joseph, who came out of enslavement to redeem his people,
and from Jonah, who emerged from the belly of the great fish with
truth that saved a city, from a dozen impetuous disciples and from
a Roman cross and from an empty tomb and from Paul, whose im-
prisonment in Rome opened not only the way to brave but a worldwide way for the gospel. It echoes from the fall of Jerusalem, which
spread the flame of the gospel throughout the Roman Empire. It
echoes from the martyrdom of the early Christians, whose blood
became the seed of the church, from the fall of Rome, after which
the victorious barbarian tribes were in turn vanquished by the

gospel, carrying its message across Europe. And it echoes even from the too-short life of a precious anacephalic child named Katie who never sat up or said "Mamma."

When Katie Burchett died, I officiated her funeral and read these amazing words from her father Dave:

Katie . . . why did you live? Maybe to help give me new inspiration to make my life count. To not let little obstacles and weaknesses keep me from reaching my God-given potential. Katie, I'll dedicate to you all the abilities that I possess. I never will tolerate myself or others wasting those precious gifts that you lacked. The ability to learn, to love, to live. I know that I have an empathy for others that I could not have possessed without your life and death. I feel more fully alive having experienced the ultimate joy of your birth and the sadness of your affliction. . . I will never be the same. You've given us hope for tomorrow. That someday we can see you whole and complete and you can meet the mommy and daddy and brothers that loved you just as you were. . . You'll always be beautiful in my mind, just like you were as a baby. Just like your mommy. But I promise you one thing, Katie. Mommy and I aren't sorry you came. We wouldn't change a thing. You see, you've done more in your short life than some people accomplish in a lifetime. Your mommy and I think that Katie is a wonderful name for an angel, because that's what you'll always be to us. God rest your soul, Katie, and know that your life counted.[2]

Faith Stands Up in Intimidating Times

In his own inimitable way, Dave Barry defines some common intimidating situations many of us frequently face: "All of us are

born with a set of instinctive fears—of falling, of the dark, of lobsters, of falling on lobsters in the dark, or speaking before a Rotary
Club, and of the words 'Some Assembly Required.'"[3] But every so
often, like David hearing Goliath's vile verbal onslaught at Elah,
we must endure dreadful giants that are many times more fearful
than just falling in the dark. Some of these are societal/cultural
giants that we face as the church in our modern-day American
context, from the increasing secularization of our society to the
outright, fearless hostility toward Christian beliefs. Others are
more personal giants that we face as individuals—job loss, sickness, death of a loved one, family strain, and financial crises.

From the outset of this book, my goal has been to show you
that courage and bravery through the Spirit are needed for facing
both the cultural and personal giants. The way to brave is about
fighting both types of giants with courage. In order to do that,
we need a David faith that stands up, an intrepid faith that bears
up. That adjective "intrepid" means resolutely fearless and dauntless, as in "an intrepid explorer"—brave, courageous, and bold.
You can see why the British Navy christened no less than eight
of their battleships with this name, "HMS Intrepid," beginning in
1747. They were launching ships that would be steady and strong
through whatever deadly intimidation that storms and tsunamis
and enemy ships threw at them. That's what Christ wants for all of
us, His people—that the testing of our faith will enable us to sail
forward through our lives, not paralyzed but boldly active, not
imprisoned by dreadful intimidation but confident in good cheer,
not frumpy but fun, not fearless but intrepid.

Such will be the reality if we allow the testing of our faith to
build into our hearts the two habits of highly intrepid people like
David. The first of these we see in David's life, not only when his
faith stood up in the Valley of Elah, but much later when, as the

king, he faced the intimidation of a coup attempt by his own son Absalom, who had "stole[n] the hearts of the people of Israel" (2 Sam. 15:6). In that desperate time, David wrote the third psalm, which begins with these words:

> LORD, how many are my foes! How many rise up against me! Many are saying of me, "God will not deliver him." But you, LORD, are a shield around me, my glory, the One who lifts my head high. I call out to the LORD, and he answers me from his holy mountain. I lie down and sleep; I wake again, because the LORD sustains me. I will not fear though tens of thousands assail me on every side. (Ps. 3:1–6)

Do you see the first habit of a highly intrepid person? They immediately focus on the presence of God when fighting their fear, thus enabling their faith to stand up. That's the very first thing you and I should do in intimidating circumstances on the way to brave, and perhaps a great strategy for starters is recalling and reciting to ourselves verses like these:

> "Be strong and courageous. Do not be afraid or terrified because of them, for the LORD your God goes with you; he will never leave you nor forsake you." (Deut. 31:6)

> Even though I walk through the valley of the shadow of death, I will fear no evil, for you are with me; your rod and your staff, they comfort me. (Ps. 23:4 ESV)

> God is our refuge and strength, an ever-present help in trouble. Therefore we will not fear, though the earth give way and the mountains fall into the heart of the sea, though its waters

roar and foam and the mountains quake with their surging. (Ps. 46:1–3)

When we frail human beings fail to focus on God's presence with us in the midst of intimidating times, we pray without faith, worship without awe, serve without joy, and suffer without hope. The result is a life of stagnation and fear, a loss of vision, an inability to persevere through intimidation. But when we realize that God has promised to be our refuge and strength, an ever-present help in trouble, our faith stands up like Martin Luther's at the Diet of Worms in 1521. The Holy Roman Emperor Charles V put the great reformer on trial in an effort to make him repudiate all his books and commit himself to silence about the gospel questions on which he had been challenging the Roman Catholic Church. Charles essentially wanted to intimidate Martin into silence. But keenly aware of God's presence and help in that pressure-packed moment, he nevertheless famously responded to the Emperor with words that got him excommunicated and further endangered his life: "Unless you prove to me by Scripture and plain reason that I am wrong, I cannot and will not recant. My conscience is captive to the Word of God. To go against conscience is neither right nor safe. Here I stand; there is nothing else I can do. God help me, amen."

> **When we frail human beings fail to focus on God's presence with us in the midst of intimidating times, we pray without faith, worship without awe, serve without joy, and suffer without hope.**

The second habit of highly intrepid people in intimidating times is not only to focus on the presence of God, but to depend on the help of God. Like five-year-old Johnny who was in the kitchen with his mom as she made supper. She asked him to go into the pantry and get her a can of tomato soup, but he didn't want to go alone. "It's dark in there and I'm scared." She said, "It's okay. Jesus will help you." Johnny walked hesitantly to the door and slowly opened it. He peeked inside, saw it was dark, and said, "Jesus, if You're in there, would You please hand me a can of tomato soup?" That's essentially David's prayer in the intimidating time when he fled Absalom's coup. "Arise, LORD! Deliver me, my God! Strike all my enemies on the jaw; break the teeth of the wicked. From the LORD comes deliverance. May your blessing be on your people" (Ps. 3:7–8). David is basically saying, "Lord, would you please hand me a can of tomato soup?"

David had settled beyond any shadow of a doubt that God was with him, "a shield around me, my glory, the One who lifts my head high." Now he was trusting the God who was with him to "catch" him, to help him by taking hold of his hand as per Isaiah, "For I am the LORD your God who takes hold of your right hand and says to you, Do not fear; I will help you" (Isa. 41:13). So must we trust God in intimidating times to help us by taking our hands, catching us, as in Henri Nouwen's beautiful quotation of a trapeze artist.

"As a flyer, I must have complete trust in my catcher. The public might think that I am the great star of the trapeze, but the real star is Joe, my catcher. He has to be there for me with split-second precision and grab me out of the air as I come to him in the long jump." "How does it work?" I asked. "The secret," he said, "is that the flyer does nothing and the catcher does everything. When I fly to Joe, I have simply to stretch out my arms and hands and wait for him to catch me and pull me safely over the apron behind the catch bar." "You do nothing!" I said, surprised. "Nothing," he answered. "The worst thing a flyer can do is try to catch the catcher. I am not supposed to catch Joe. It's Joe's task to catch me. If I grabbed Joe's wrists, I might break them, or he might break mine, and that would be the end for both of us. A flyer must fly, and a catcher must catch, and the flyer must trust, with outstretched arms, that his catcher will be there for him."[4]

That's what thirty-nine-year-old Pastor Evan Mawarire did one day last year when he made a four-minute video critical of Robert Mugabe—one of the world's most corrupt and oppressive dictators in history—with the flag of desperately poor and looted (by Mugabe) Zimbabwe wrapped around his neck. Evan pointed out that the colors of that flag have meaning. "For example, red is supposed to stand for the blood that patriots shed in the liberation effort. But what would those patriots say about Zimbabwe now? What had they died for? That's the kind of thing Mawarire asked in his video. At the end of it, he asked Zimbabweans to stand up: for themselves, for their flag, and for their country." The next morning, the video had gone viral. Striking a nerve among Zimbabweans, it led to a democracy movement fueled by twenty-five more videos that travel under a hashtag, #ThisFlag.

Later there was a mass protest in Zimbabwe and, six days afterwards, Evan Mawarire was arrested for "incitement to violence." The courthouse for Mawarire's hearing was packed with people singing worship songs, along with thousands outside. "Mawarire could hear it from his prison cell. . . . While in the dock, Mawarire got a rude, frightening surprise: The charge against him had been changed to what amounted to treason. He looked at his wife and mouthed, 'I'm sorry.' . . . There was a break in the hearing. Night had fallen. Outside the courthouse, people were lighting candles, and singing. They were also buying food for one another. Again, the guards marveled, telling the prisoner in his cell about the scene. Back in the courtroom, the magistrate had good news: The prisoner was to be released on a technicality. . . . Mawarire fell into the arms of the waiting, weeping crowd. 'Zimbabwean flags were everywhere,' he says. From his wife, he learned some grim news: While he was in prison, thugs had tried to rape her. (She was seven months pregnant, incidentally.) They had also tried to kidnap the two kids."

Since then, Evan has been in and out of Zimbabwe and in and out of jail at the hands of Mugabe, who constantly warns Mawarire to stick to religion and not meddle in politics. Evan knows "the role of pastors in the American civil-rights movement" and so is "well aware that the foremost of those pastors, Martin Luther King, was martyred." His common response is a verse from the 27th Psalm: "I remain confident of this: I will see the goodness of the Lord in the land of the living."[5] In other words, a flyer must fly, and a catcher must catch, and Evan is trusting, with outstretched arms, that his catcher will be there for him. That's why his faith can stand up even in highly intimidating circumstances.

Faith Stands Up in Dangerous Times

A tested faith is a fearless faith that stands up in painful times and intimidating times, and yes, in dangerous times too. The star exemplar of the last category is, of course, David at Elah. When King Saul tried to talk David out of fighting Goliath by accentuating the obvious physical danger David faced of sudden, violent death at the hands of a seasoned killer, the kid gave his definitive and unanswerable reply: "'The Lord who rescued me from the paw of the lion and the paw of the bear will rescue me from the hand of this Philistine.' Saul said to David, 'Go, and the Lord be with you'" (1 Sam. 17:37). Lions and tigers and bears, oh my? No, for David it was, lions and giants and bears, okay! His faith had been tested by lion tooth and bear paw and was thereby strengthened to face the Philistine giant. That's what gave David the calm confidence to make the following giggle-producing prediction to Goliath's face: "This very day I will give the carcasses of the Philistine army to the birds and the wild animals, and *the whole world will know that there is a God in Israel.* All those gathered here will know that it is not by sword or spear that the Lord saves; for the battle is the Lord's, and he will give all of you into our hands" (1 Sam. 17:46–47). What happened next after David's faith stood up is the stuff of legend.

With etiquette thus observed, David got on with it sans hesitation. He ran at Goliath, scooping a stone into his sling and letting it fly in one smooth motion (like on December 28, 1975, when Roger Staubach threw his famous Hail Mary pass to Drew Pearson with only thirty-two seconds left in the game to beat the Minnesota Vikings in a divisional playoff game, but I digress). At thirty-four feet per second, David's projectile effectively flat-footed the giant, who could only wonder at his approaching demise. Bullseye! Goliath's last thought, unfortunately, was an incomplete sentence. "What's that crazy adolescent think he's doi—?" Hence did Goliath get stoned out of his mind, the saying "the bigger they are the harder they fall" get born, and the shepherd boy, against all the Las Vegas bookmakers' odds, get famous for slam-dunking a giant. So, an archaeologist found a sarcophagus containing a mummy in the Negev Desert and called the curator of a prestigious museum. "I've got the three-thousand-year-old mummy of a man who died of heart failure!" he exclaimed.

The curator replied, "Bring him in. We'll check it out." A week later, the amazed curator called the archaeologist. "You were right about the mummy's cause of death. How did you know?" The archaeologist replied, "Easy. There was a piece of paper in his hand that read, '10,000 shekels on Goliath.'" (Just kidding, but not about the long-shot nature of David's prediction to the giant . . .)

David ran to the prone Hulkster, borrowed his sword, thanks very much, and removed his head with due flourish. And all this before lunch! Not a bad day's work, all things considered. David's besting of Goliath in Elah did not go unobserved, and its ramifications were immediate. Having witnessed the steel backbone of a shepherd lad in defeating the giant, each of the formerly timid Israelite soldiers acquired one of their own. With David's beheading of Goliath as the starter's gun, God's army pursued and decisively defeated the pagan army. That's how the fledgling Israelite nation was saved. And that's how a skinny kid's courage in facing down the terrorizer of his nation became a legendary metaphor for intrepid faith, unlikely heroism, and undaunted courage. If the USA's gold medal victory over the Soviets in the 1980 Olympic Games is rightfully called "The Miracle on Ice," then surely David's victory over the Philistine giant circa 800 BC could rightfully be called "The Miracle in Elah." The son of Jesse's undisputed heroism became immediately legendary, and the words "David and Goliath" an instantly recognizable phrase to this day, symbolizing unmitigated courage.[6]

The beautiful thing about a tested faith on display is the effect on others who might still be sidelined by their fear. I love the end

> **The beautiful thing about a tested faith on display is the effect on others who might still be sidelined by their fear.**

of the story about David's faith standing up in a time of great danger. Having slain Goliath in full view of an utterly amazed Israelite army, the victorious David had a powerful effect on the other soldiers: "Then the men of Israel and Judah surged forward with a shout and pursued the Philistines . . . [and] plundered their camp" (1 Sam. 17:52–53). Israel found courage to enter the Valley of Elah *after* their champion won victory in the Valley of Elah! They didn't fight *for* victory that day, but *from* victory. They didn't gin up their own courage, but walked in the courage of their champion, who also didn't gin up his own courage. Rather, David focused on God's presence and relied on God's help as he had during previous times of danger populated with lions and bears.

That's precisely what German theologian and churchman Dietrich Bonhoeffer did early on the morning of April 9, 1945, as he was executed in Flossenbürg concentration camp for his part in a conspiracy to assassinate Adolph Hitler. The camp doctor described the scene: "Pastor Bonhoeffer, before taking off his prison garb, knelt on the floor praying fervently to his God. I was most deeply moved by the way this lovable man prayed, so devout and so certain that God heard his prayer. At the place of execution he again said a short prayer and then climbed up the steps of the gallows, brave and composed . . . I have hardly ever seen a man die so entirely submissive to he will of God."

As remarkable a scene as that was, even more remarkable was that Bonhoeffer easily could have avoided it. In November of 1938, the infamous Kristallnacht (Night of Broken Glass) was organized by Nazis against Germany's Jews. Seeing the danger, Bonhoeffer sailed to the United States in June of 1939 with thoughts of emigration. But escaping to safety when his countrymen faced danger did not sit well with him. On July 8, 1939, Bonhoeffer sailed straight back into the hell that Germany had become, back into danger and possible death. His own words tell us where he found courage to return: "Daring to do what is right, not what fancy may tell you, valiantly grasping occasions, not cravenly doubting—freedom comes only through deeds, not through thoughts taking wing. Faint not nor fear, but go out to the storm and the action, trusting in God whose commandment you faithfully follow; freedom, exultant, will welcome your spirit with joy."[7]

Yes, it will, for the fruit of prevailing in the storm is a steadfast confidence in facing battles small and large. So lions and tigers and bears (and giants), okay! Because faith stood up, it has exultant freedom to stand up. On your way to brave, may this be your story too.

Section 5

GOD TRAINS US

1 SAMUEL 17:48–50

As the Philistine moved closer
to attack him, David ran quickly
toward the battle line to meet him.
Reaching into his bag and taking
out a stone, he slung it and struck
the Philistine on the forehead. The
stone sank into his forehead, and
he fell facedown on the ground.
So David triumphed over the
Philistine with a sling and a stone;
without a sword in his hand he
struck down the Philistine and
killed him.

AS A SHEPHERD DETERMINED to protect his sheep, David diligently practiced the craft of the sling. And as a result of his focused training, David acquired great skill, marked by power and accuracy with his weapon, that made him lethal to enemies of the flock. In those days, skilled shepherds like David could hit a pigeon in flight at thirty yards with stones the size of baseballs that they fired at over 100 mph. That's why "slingers" were used in ancient armies much like artillery in modern warfare. They were not only accurate with slings and stones. They were *deadly* accurate with slings and stones!

David fished out his little sling which, compared to the swords and spears and standards of the surrounding soldiers, looked pitiful and paltry. But David's training with sling and stone to protect sheep from predators was God's strategy to grant him the confidence necessary to protect people from giants. "From tending the sheep he brought him to be the shepherd of his people Jacob, of Israel his inheritance. And David shepherded them with integrity of heart; with skillful hands he led them" (Ps. 78:71–72).

Training, then, made David brave. And it will make us brave too as we Christ followers grow skilled in handling our most powerful spiritual weapon, as described by Paul the apostle. "In addition to all this, take up the shield of faith, with which you can extinguish all the flaming arrows of the evil one. Take the helmet of salvation and the Sword of the Spirit, which is the Word of God" (Eph. 6:16–17). Diligent training in knowing and living out of that Word of God will likewise put us on the way to brave as it shapes in us a David faith for a Goliath world.

Chapter 9

EAT THIS BOOK

When your words came, I ate them; they were my joy and my heart's delight.
—JEREMIAH 15:16

There's nothing like the written Word of God for . . . training us to live
God's way. Through the Word we are put together and shaped up for
the tasks God has for us. —2 TIMOTHY 3:16-17 MSG

A huge component of David's courage in facing Goliath was the
confidence he derived from his focused training with sling and
stone—the shepherd's weapon of choice. The great skill that David
acquired through diligent practice resulted in lethal power, deadly
accuracy, and definitive victory when he faced the enemy. Paul the
apostle describes our version of David's "sling and stone" as Christ
followers today. "In addition to all this, take up . . . the sword of
the Spirit, which is the word of God" (Eph. 6:16–17). Listed with
the spiritual "armor of God," the Holy Scriptures appear to be the
only offensive weapon in the Christian's spiritual arsenal. But that's
okay. David had only a sling, but that was weapon enough. We
have only the Word, but that's weapon enough as well.

Jesus proved that in His great confrontation with Satan in the
wilderness just prior to His baptism by John and the beginning of
His earthly ministry. See Christ's definitive victory when he coun-
tered the temptations of the devil in the wilderness by wielding
the sword of the Spirit (a.k.a. the Word of God).

The devil said to him, "If you are the Son of God, tell this stone to become bread." *Jesus answered, "It is written: 'Man shall not live on bread alone.'"* The devil led him up to a high place and showed him in an instant all the kingdoms of the world. And he said to him, "I will give you all their authority and splendor; it has been given to me, and I can give it to anyone I want to. If you worship me, it will all be yours." *Jesus answered, "It is written: 'Worship the Lord your God and serve him only.'"* The devil led him to Jerusalem and had him stand on the highest point of the temple. "If you are the Son of God," he said, "throw yourself down from here. For it is written: 'He will command his angels concerning you to guard you carefully; they will lift you up in their hands, so that you will not strike your foot against a stone.'" *Jesus answered, "It is said: 'Do not put the Lord your God to the test.'"* When the devil had finished all this tempting, he left him until an opportune time. (Luke 4:3–13)

So marinated in the Word of God (particularly Deuteronomy 6 and 8) was Jesus' heart and soul and mind that Satan could not deter His purpose, short-circuit His mission, or derail His ministry with veiled threats, illicit riches, or forbidden power. Jesus prevailed on the way to brave because of His skill with the sword of the Spirit, the Word of God. So shall we too if we become proficient in handling the Holy Scriptures.

As my three girls and two boys (whose births spanned twelve years) were growing up, I desperately wanted them to accept God's invitation to the courage and comfort implicit in the counsel of His Word. Only one problem. They were too young to read, much less grasp the theological significance of immersing themselves in Scripture! I solved this problem by starting a journal for each of them when they were just toddlers and presented it to them on the evening that Alice and I moved them into their dorm rooms to start college (after making a copy of course!). That way I could write to each one adult-to-adult years before they even reached puberty and know that they would later receive my words at an opportune time. Here's a passage from my first son's journal (who, by the way, is twenty-seven years old as of this writing).

8/28/91
Dear Jonathan,
You're a strapping 2 ½ year-old so full of curiosity and energy that at times you nearly burst (and me along with you!). You're obviously a natural athlete. And you're mischievous. And your little heart is just huge! All signs of a leader who I am already convinced is going to cut a wide swath through this old world for God's Kingdom. Jonathan, I can't wait to see what significant parts God has for you to play one day in this grand adventure!

In this quest Jonathan I want you always to have an anchor in your life—a reference point to define your values and chart your course and encourage your heart. That's the Word of God. Learn to delight in God's ways as revealed in The Book, and you'll never be lost as are so many poor, misguided wasters of life in this world! Remember 2 Peter 1.20–21 when your faith in scripture needs bolstering: "No prophecy of scripture came about by the prophet's own interpretation. For prophecy never had its origin in the will of man, but men spoke from God as they were carried along by His Holy Spirit." God is obviously infinitely smarter than we are, so we're never smarter than when we listen to Him and do it His way! As the Great Reformer Martin Luther said:

"Oh! How great and glorious a thing it is to have before me the Word of God! He who loses sight of [it] falls into despair; he follows only the disorderly tendency of his heart and of the world's vanity, which lead him on to destruction."

The history of the world is a case in point of that last line. But my son, you and I don't have to learn this the hard way. Thank God!

Love always Laddie,
Dad

David prevailed over Goliath in the Valley of Elah through his skill with his weapon of choice—a sling. But internally, he wielded another weapon even more powerful than the sling. "Your word is a lamp for my feet, a light on my path . . . My heart is set on keeping your decrees to the very end" (Ps. 119:105, 112). So Jesus prevailed over Satan in the Wilderness of Sin through his skill with that same weapon of choice, God's Word. So I trusted as well that my children and I would prevail on the way to brave by becoming proficient in wielding the Scriptures.

How God's Word Trains Us

Writing to a young pastor in a daunting first-century predicament, the great apostle Paul gives the most succinct description of how such training in the Scriptures develops David faith for our Goliath world.

But as for you, continue in what you have learned and have become convinced of, because you know those from whom you learned it, and how from infancy you have known the Holy Scriptures, which are able to make you wise for salvation through faith in Christ Jesus. All Scripture is God-breathed and is useful for teaching, rebuking, correcting and training in righteousness, so that the servant of God may be thoroughly equipped for every good work. (2 Tim. 3:14–17)

Let's look at why all who want to walk in the way of brave must "eat this book."[1]

The phrase "All Scripture is God-breathed" comes from a single Greek word (*theopneustos*), which literally means "exhaled by God." Not "God-shouted" or "God-dictated," but God-breathed! As Peter observes, men wrote the Scriptures "as they were moved by the Holy Spirit" (2 Peter 1:21 NKJV). So the scriptural claim is that what God wanted written flowed with supernatural inspiration and precision through the personalities of over forty different authors over a span of 1,500 years in three different ancient written languages.

Paul refers to Scripture as "the word of truth" (2 Tim. 2:15). Truth is a broad category that I'll break down into two components—*empirical* truth and *comprehensive* truth. Empirical truth is the stuff of scientific measurement and mathematics and the laboratory. It's true that water boils at 212°F and freezes at 32°F and that $2 + 2 = 4$. That's empirical, repeatable, unarguable fact. But empirical truth doesn't go beyond the observable features of our universe to answer questions that all of us have, like "Who *made* water and *established* the parameters of its boiling and freezing points, and for what ultimate purpose?" Even with a growing body of scientific empirical truth, we humans live in a dark place with a deep need for comprehensive truth that helps us understand our purpose and place in the universe. Voila! For this reason, God has "breathed out" the Scripture, which the apostle Peter strongly encourages us to hold in very high regard. "We also have the prophetic message as something completely reliable, and you will do well to pay attention to it, as to a light shining in a dark place, until the day dawns and the morning star rises in your hearts" (2 Peter 1:19).

When we regularly take in the truth of God's story, we enjoy a spiritual feast for our souls, which literally transforms our lives. That, functionally, is what the Bible is to Christians—a spiritual feast. And we're invited to dig in! "'Son of man, eat this scroll I am giving you and fill your stomach with it.' So I ate it, and it tasted as sweet as honey in my mouth" (Ezek. 3:3). Picture God as heaven's Iron Chef and the Bible as a smorgasbord of his most delectable culinary creations. And hear His invitation: "Taste and see that the LORD is good" (Ps. 34:8). We don't just eat the book because it tastes good, though. We eat it because it's true, and truth is the basic requirement for any life—to be fully lived! As Jesus said: "It is written: 'Man shall not live on bread alone, but on every word that comes from the mouth of God'" (Matt. 4:4).

Paul continues to explain how God's Word trains us. "All Scripture is God-breathed and is useful for . . . rebuking" (2 Tim. 3:16). Paul uses the word *elegchos*, which here means to "rebuke or convict." As sin-broken human beings living in a sin-broken creation, it's difficult for us to walk in the way of brave without the Word of God "exposing our rebellion" (2 Tim. 3:16 MSG) because we don't naturally see our rebellion for what it really is. We think "the way it is" (and the way we are) is good and normal and rational and that it is thereby "the way it ought to be" (and the way we were always meant to be).

But if we believe that, we are mistaken in the same way that people are mistaken who believe that the US standard railroad gauge—4 feet 8.5 inches being the distance between rails—is good and normal and rational and "the way it ought to be" and "was always meant to be." After all, when NASA engineers ship the solid rocket boosters (or SRBs, which attach to the sides of the main fuel tank) to the space shuttle launch pad on Merritt Island in Florida from the Thiokol factory in Utah, they do it on US standard railroad gauge. But that's an odd number: 4 feet 8.5 inches. Why that precise distance? Because that's the way they built rails in England, and English expatriates built US railroads. Why did the English build them like that? Because their first rail lines were built by the same people who built the pre-railroad tramways, and that's the gauge *they* used. But why that particular gauge? Because the people who built the tramways used the same jigs and tools that they used for building wagons whose wheels would break on some of the old, long-distance roads in England if they didn't match up to the spacing of the wheel ruts. Let's press on! Who built those old roads in England? Imperial Rome, for its legions. And the ruts in those Roman roads? Formed by chariots constructed at exactly 4 feet, 8.5 inches in width to accommodate the rear ends of two Roman warhorses! How frustrating that must have been two thousand years later to the engineers who designed the space shuttle's SRBs. They would have preferred to make them a bit fatter, but couldn't because they knew the SRBs had to be shipped by train from the factory through a tunnel in the mountains to the launch site on rails designed, not to accommodate rocket engines, but two horses' behinds.[2]

Here is the ultimate value of the written Word of God in "exposing our rebellion" (2 Tim. 3:16 MSG). Seeing the reality that our present predicament as human beings is *not* natural and normal and rational and good but is instead caused by rebellion enables us to escape denial and build a better life on the firm foundation of truth. It frees us from such common deceptions as the perfectibility of mankind, the innate goodness of human beings, and the

When the Word of God exposes the rebellion of those deceptions, we can go back and build the railroad of our future lives with a gauge designed for rocket boosters and not horses' derrieres, for intrepid disciples and not self-deceived pretenders.

relativity of moral values, which function like ancient jigs and tools that lock future technology into ancient and outmoded ways. When the Word of God exposes the rebellion of those deceptions, we can go back and build the railroad of our future lives with a gauge designed for rocket boosters and not horses' derrieres, for intrepid disciples and not self-deceived pretenders. That's why Paul the apostle was so insistent on Christ followers embracing Scripture, which exposes human rebellion.

> For I do not want you to be ignorant of the fact, brothers and sisters, that our ancestors were all under the cloud and that they all passed through the sea. They were all baptized into Moses in the cloud and in the sea. They all ate the same spiritual food and drank the same spiritual drink; for they drank from the spiritual rock that accompanied them, and that rock was Christ. Nevertheless, God was not pleased with most of them; their bodies were scattered in the wilderness. Now these things occurred as examples to keep us from setting our hearts on evil things as they did. (1 Cor. 10:1–6)

Now the exposure of our rebellion is often painful, "For the word of God is alive and active. Sharper than any double-edged sword, it penetrates even to dividing soul and spirit, joints and marrow; it judges the thoughts and attitudes of the heart" (Heb.

4:12). Mark Twain once quipped, "Most people are bothered by those passages of Scripture they do *not* understand, but the passages that bother me are those I *do* understand." He had obviously felt the pain of God's double-edged sword. But the pain of exposure is beneficial because it keeps us from repeating humankind's past mistakes. To continue with Paul, "These things happened to them as examples and were written down as warnings for us, on whom the culmination of the ages has come. So, if you think you are standing firm, be careful that you don't fall!" (1 Cor. 10:11–12).

The only question for those of us who want to walk in the way of brave is this: Will we welcome the pain implicit in the Scripture's exposure of our rebellion and be thereby warned and set free from the bonds of humankind's past mistakes? Or, will we reject the pain and ignore the Scripture's exposure of our rebellion so that we can continue unfettered in it? I hope we all choose the former, as did Aurelius in fourth century North Africa. He was a young scholar using the "US Standard Railroad Gauge" to search for the true, the good, and the beautiful by reading philosophy in the day and chasing wild women and wine in the night. But the double-minded deception of that faulty moral greatly frustrated Aurelius and launched him on a desperate search for resolution. One day upon retreating to a small garden for reflection, he reported this famous experience.

> Then a huge storm rose up within me bringing with it a huge downpour of tears. Suddenly a voice reaches my ears . . . the voice of a boy or a girl . . . and in a kind of singsong the words are constantly repeated: "Take it and read it. [*tolle lege*]" . . . I must interpret this as a divine command to me to open the book and read . . . I snatched up the book, opened it, and

read in silence the passage upon which my eyes first fell. "Not in rioting and drunkenness, not in chambering and wantonness, not in strife and envying; but put ye on the Lord Jesus first, and make not provision for the flesh in concupiscence." I had no wish to read further; there was no need to. For immediately when I had reached the end of this sentence it was as though my heart was filled with a light of confidence and all the shadows of my doubt were swept away.[3]

Thus the turning point in the life of Aurelius Augustine (who later would become the Bishop of Hippo and one of the most influential theologians in all of Christian history) came at the very moment when he discovered "there's nothing like the written Word of God for . . . *exposing our rebellion*" (2 Tim. 3:15–16 MSG). But Paul has more.

The Bible *is* "101 Ways to Build a Boat" for those marooned on this spiritual desert island of a planet we're on! We are all washed up here like spiritual castaways, desperately needing answers to the big questions of life.

"All Scripture is God-breathed and is useful for . . . correcting" (2 Tim. 3:16). The original word Paul used for "correcting"[4] means "restore to an upright state." Bible truth forces us back to reality by exposing our rebellion (painful!) and then restores us to an upright state by getting us back on the right track (hopeful!) as we read it not just purposefully but even desperately ("Take and read" [*tolle lege*] . . . like Augustine).

G. K. Chesterton was a British Christian writer and apologist famous for his quick wit. A reporter once asked him what one book he would want with him if he found himself stranded on a deserted island. The reporter suggested Chesterton might want the Bible or Shakespeare or perhaps a novel by Dickens? Chesterton famously replied: "101 Ways to Build a Boat." The genius of that answer was that the Bible *is* "101 Ways to Build a Boat" for those marooned on this spiritual desert island of a planet we're on! We are all washed up here like spiritual castaways, desperately needing answers to the big questions of life. For us, God's great gift is a book that answers those questions and brings us deliverance!

One day I received notice that I had a package at the post office. So on my lunch hour, I went there and stood in front of the Dutch door where people pick up their packages. There's a permanent sign over a button by that usually closed door that reads: "Push the button for service, and please allow time for the attendant to respond before pushing the button again." So I dutifully pushed the button, and waited . . . a long time, at least five minutes! Then pushed again, and waited another five again, then pushed again! One of the clerks behind the counter saw me stalking around the package door. She came behind and opened it with a sign in her hand, which she wordlessly taped over the permanent "push the button" sign. It read: "Buzzer is broken. Please knock loudly for service." Then she turned and said to me. "Why do you keep pushing the button when the buzzer is broken?" (Um, maybe because nobody posted the sign telling me the buzzer was broken?) Thank God for posting that sign for the world. It's His Word that tells us that the human buzzer is broken. It's His Word that corrects our futile and frustrating efforts to live life according to the US Standard Railroad Gauge.

I heard of a South Sea Islander who proudly displayed his Bible to an American G.I. during WWII. He had received it as a present from a missionary many years before and actually read it and had his life transformed by it. The soldier said, "O, my friends and I have outgrown that sort of thing." The Islander smiled and said, "Well, it's a good thing we haven't, because if it weren't for this book, you would be our evening meal." That man and his people had discovered that there's no book like the Bible for exposing rebellion and correcting mistakes!

Finally Paul concludes, "All Scripture is breathed out by God and profitable for teaching, for reproof, for correction, and for training in righteousness, that the man of God may be complete, equipped for every good work" (2 Tim. 3:16–17 ESV). The word Paul used for "training" (*paideia*) here described the work of the *paedogogos*, a teacher who accompanied and taught a child in all places whether at school, gymnasium, home, or market. God trains us through His Word so that we might be "complete" (*artios*) and "equipped" as suitable vessels for His work! The word Paul uses for "equipped" (*exartizo*) means "completely outfitted, fully furnished." It was used to describe a seaworthy, fully supplied boat. Like an escape boat for castaways, a way off Chesterton's island? Yes! The Bible shapes us up for the tasks God has for us, but only if we let its truth train us to live God's way.

I periodically make the same mistake, not by sitting needlessly on an island with a satellite phone unopened in a FedEx box, but by sitting needlessly on a spiritual deserted island with a package from God, the Bible, unopened.

During Superbowl XXXVII, a FedEx commercial spoofed the movie *Cast Away*, in which Tom Hanks played a FedEx worker whose plane went down, stranding him on a desert island for years. Looking like the bedraggled Hanks in the movie, the FedEx employee in the commercial goes to the door of a suburban home, package in hand. When a lady comes to the door, he explains that he survived five years on the island, and during that whole time he kept this package to deliver it to her. She says, "Thank you." But he is curious. "By the way, what's in the package?" She opens it saying, "Nothing really, just a satellite phone, GPS locator, fishing rod, water purifier, and some seeds." I love the look on the guy's face while she's ticking this stuff off—it portrays pure incredulous kicking-himself regret and remorse. He's thinking, "You mean I sat on that rock when, if I'd only opened this stupid box, I could have been home five years ago?!" Yep. That's right.

I don't know about you, but I periodically make the same mistake, not by sitting needlessly on an island with a satellite phone unopened in a FedEx box, but by sitting needlessly on a spiritual deserted island with a package from God, the Bible, unopened. Peter says that in that Bible are God's "very great and precious promises, so that through them you may participate in the divine nature" (2 Peter 1:4). What a FedEx package! Have you opened it yet? As Eugene Peterson observes,

> Christians feed on Scripture. Holy Scripture nurtures the holy community as food nurtures the human body. Christians don't simply learn or study or use Scripture; we assimilate it, take it into our lives in such a way that it gets metabolized into acts of love, cups of cold water, missions into all the world, healing and evangelism and justice in Jesus' name, hands raised in adoration of the Father, feet washed in company with the Son.[5]

God's Word is filled with the finest food for hungry souls. Time to eat this book!

Covered by His Dust

Being trained in the Word of God means more than just knowing the Word. It means living it. Living the Word means becoming like Jesus, who is, according to John 1, *the* Word. In other words, they would be "covered by his dust," as the saying went in Jesus' day, when rabbis selected disciples to train with them 24/7 under their particular interpretive school, or "yoke." From that moment, the disciples' entire lives were dedicated to emulating their master as they *followed his teaching* down the dusty roads of their lives. Hence family and friends would send them off with this blessing: "May you be covered in the dust of your rabbi." May *we* be covered by the dust of *ours* as well!

But that will only happen if we are determined to make it happen, because being covered by Jesus' dust is not a convenient, one-and-done proposition. It takes time and applied determination to "eat this book" systematically, comprehensively, and effectively. The particular approach to knowing and living the Word of God that I have always found beneficial is the discipline of meditation (also called "Lectio Divina" or "divine reading"), which I apply to a daily Bible reading plan (many of which are available in print or in Bible Applications such as the excellent YouVersion). Quite simply, "Lectio" entails five movements, which I remember as the "5 Rs."

1. **Reading**: *read* the text slowly and silently.
2. **Reflecting**: *listen* to what the text is saying to you, yielded and still.
3. **Responding**: *turn* your reflection into a short *prayer* of submission, confession, faith, or obedience.

4. **Resting:** *read* the text again while resting in the *truth* of who God is and who He has created you to be.

5. **Resolving:** *live* out the text as a personal word to the particular circumstances of your everyday life.

That's a deceptively simple approach for getting into Scripture as a Christ follower. It seems easy because the methodology is simple and intuitive. But it's not easy because the effort and time required is costly. But whatever price we must pay to be covered by Christ's dust is more than worth our sustained focus and application. As Paul wrote from a Roman jail, "But one thing I do: Forgetting what is behind and straining toward what is ahead, I press on toward the goal to win the prize for which God has called me heavenward in Christ Jesus" (Phil. 3:13–14). The original word Paul uses for "straining toward" (*epekteino*) pictures the body of a runner in the ancient Isthmian games making the final "lean" to win his race. For emphasis, the text literally says, "Toward the goal, I press on."

That's what Shun Fujimoto, a Japanese gymnast in the 1976 Olympics in Montreal, did after he broke his right knee during the floor exercises. It was obvious to all that he would be forced to withdraw. But on the following day, Fujimoto competed in his strongest event, the rings. His routine was excellent, but the critical point lay ahead—the dismount. Without hesitation, Fujimoto ended with a twisting, triple somersault. There was a moment of intense quiet as he landed with tremendous impact on his wounded knee. Then came thundering applause as he stood his ground. Later, reporters asked about that moment and he replied, "The pain shot through me like a knife. It brought tears to my eyes. But now I have a gold medal and the pain is gone."

That's what I wanted to communicate to my little boy those

years ago in his journal. The "pain" of discipline and focused effort in immersing our hearts and souls and minds in the truth of God's Word throughout the decades of our lives is quickly assuaged when the dust of our Master begins to cover us.

September 1, 2007

Hey Jono,

Ask the famous people of our day what life's most important asset is, and you'll get varied responses. Playboys would say "Lots of sex." Entrepreneurs would say, "Lots of money." Narcissists would say, "Lots of attention." Certain politicians would say, "Lots of power." But look in God's word, and you'll discover these all would be dead wrong. What is life's most important asset? The answer is in Psalm 112. "Blessed is the man who fears the Lord, who finds great delight in His commands" (verse 1).

Jono, the blessing of God on your life is your life's greatest asset, bar none. The operative question, then, is this: how does a person live in such a way as to elicit God's blessing? Answer: fear God. That just means taking Him seriously enough to listen to what He says in His Word, and do it. Now I know that the simplicity of that statement belies the difficulty of its execution. Hiding God's Word in your heart requires time and study and self-discipline and systematic, daily effort. And that's not just for a few days or weeks or months or years. That's for your whole life on this planet! Whoa! A big ask, I know, but eminently worth it because of what God promises to all those who "find great delight in his commands":

First, a legacy that endures! "His children will be mighty in the land; the generation of the upright will be blessed. Wealth and riches are in his house and his righteousness endures forever" (verse 2). The wealth here is not necessarily of the monetary kind. It's joy, pride in one another, the satisfaction of making a difference, doing good changing the world. You leave a legacy of influence and inspiration in the lives of all those you influence, beginning with your children, but going out from there in ripples of respect.

Second, hope that overcomes. "Even in darkness light dawns for the upright, for the gracious and compassionate and righteous man. Good will come to him who is generous and lends freely, who conducts his affairs with justice. Surely he will never be shaken; a righteous man will be remembered forever" (verses 4-6). Does fearing God and obeying His commands insulate us from pain? No. Darkness comes even to the faithful in this broken world. It will come to you in your lifetime, Jonathan. But "even in darkness" the upright find light. Those he has helped, help. Those he has loved, love. Those to whom he's shown justice, defend. What goes around, comes around. Be an "upright" person Jonathan, and no darkness, no matter how deep, can overcome you.

Third, confidence that assures: "He will have no fear of bad news; his heart is steadfast, trusting in the Lord. His heart is secure, he will have no fear; in the end he will look in triumph on his foes. He has scattered abroad his gifts to the poor, his righteousness endures forever; his horn will be lifted high in honor" (verses 7-8). Fear is a dead give-away for going it alone. Show me someone who has walked away from the Lord, and I'll show you someone who fears what may lurk around every corner. On the other hand, show me a person who is trusting God and walking in the light of His Word and I'll show you someone who is as gold as a lion! And why would he not be? Jono, if your Guardian is the Creator of the Universe, who or what could possibly push you around? Not so, however the wicked: "The wicked man will see and be vexed he will gnash his teeth and waste away; the longings of the wicked will come to nothing" (verse 10). Jon, be blessed. Choose blessing. Reach out and receive what the Lord wants you to have! Fear Him; delight always in His commands. You'll never regret it!

> *All my Love & Blessings Jono,*
> *Dad*

Paul understood what it costs to be covered with the Master's dust, but also that elation is the reward of those who press on "toward the goal to win the prize." Gold medals have a powerful way of erasing pain. That's what David learned when standing victorious over the inert body of the giant. That's what my son learned many years after my entry in his journal above, as he stands regularly today to lead thousands in his capacity as a worship pastor. Being trained in living the Word of God as a disciple is not a singular, charismatic experience. It's an extended, personal choice to live out the Word of God in our lives with all our might while we do live! So let's take up the sword of the Spirit and walk in the way of brave by "eating this Book" and letting the beautiful dust of our Master settle upon us.

Chapter 10

THE PEOPLE
OF THE BOOK

Spiritual formation occurs primarily in the context of community. . . . Long term interpersonal relationships are the crucible of genuine progress in the Christian life. People who stay grow. People who leave do not grow . . . It is a simple but profound biblical reality that we both grow and thrive together or we do not grow much at all. —Joseph H. Hellerman, *When the Church Was a Family*

Why is community worth the bother? Why is such love necessary, as painful as it is? Apart from being commanded by God, the type of immediate, incarnational Christian experience I'm talking about must become corporate if it is ever to be sustained. The message of the early church is that "simple people could be amazingly powerful when they were members of one another".
—Gary Thomas, *The Beautiful Fight*

Surely David's courage in facing Goliath was bolstered by the confidence he'd gained by consistent training with sling and stone—his shepherd's weapon of choice. The great apostle Paul describes our New Testament Christ followers' version of David's sling and stone in his famous description of "the armor of God." "In addition to all this, take up . . . the sword of the Spirit, which is the word of God" (Eph. 6:16–17). The Holy Scriptures are the only offensive weapon in the Christian's spiritual arsenal. Extending the David analogy then, we can conclude that, to the extent that we pursue the young shepherd's disciplined training with our

weapon (the Bible) as he did with his (the sling), we will walk
with David in the way to brave. That was certainly the substance
of God's promise through Joshua to His Old Testament people.

> Be strong and very courageous. Be careful to obey all the law
> my servant Moses gave you; do not turn from it to the right or
> to the left, that you may be successful wherever you go. Keep
> this Book of the Law always on your lips; meditate on it day
> and night, so that you may be careful to do everything writ-
> ten in it. Then you will be prosperous and successful. Have I
> not commanded you? Be strong and courageous. Do not be
> afraid; do not be discouraged, for the LORD your God will be
> with you wherever you go. (Josh. 1:7–9)

The connection here between strength and courage, prosperity and success, with diligent training in and application of the
Word of God is unmistakable. So is the context and community of
that Scripture training—the community of God's people.

I love the Qur'an's primary designation of Jews and Christians
with what I consider a backhanded complimentary phrase—
"People of the Book." Muhammad was no fan of either group, but
could it be that describing them so was his admission of grudging
respect for the courage he'd observed of them first-hand to draw
from their devotion to the Old and New Testament Scriptures?
If so, this is just one more instance in which God's people have
proven that the way to brave is training in God's Word, and that
the "classroom" where that training takes place is the community
of God's people. As Joshua demonstrated in the Old Testament
and Paul in the New, the devotion of God's people to God's Book
as the organizing principle for their unity and mission planted
their feet firmly on the way to brave in the land of giants by shap-

ing them into a unique, powerful, and courageous community according to God's plan. As Christ followers moving forward today in our post-Christian America, we have no higher priority than to promote, protect, and participate in that community because, organized around the truth of Scripture, it truly is our classroom for courage.

Together We're Better

As I've attempted to show in earlier chapters, the sweep of history, the progression of Scripture, and the message of prophets and priests and Jesus Himself and reveal that the world of people that God created to be in community with Him and each other is broken by sin. It is, as John Milton described it, "paradise lost." But God has undertaken through Jesus' cross to forgive and reclaim a people who will love and follow Him and be devoted to creating foretastes of His peaceable kingdom wherever they live, work, and play.

When we do so, Peter's description of God's purpose for Christians' beautiful community becomes reality: "But you are a chosen people, a royal priesthood, a holy nation, God's special possession, *that you may declare the praises of him* who called you out of darkness into his wonderful light" (1 Peter 2:9). The beauty of the "People of the Book," as well as our boldness in declaring God's praise in the land of giants, is a direct function of our community. In other words, we Christ followers are always better *together* because our community proves to be a vital step on the way to brave.

This is only true, however, if our community is true and biblical and authentic, and not just technological connectivity. The latter is pseudocommunity in which more and more people are putting themselves into comfortable, convenient, and personally beneficial groups on Facebook and WeChat and exchanging news and information on Instagram and Twitter and SnapChat and calling all of that "community." But as former US Surgeon General Dr. Vivek H. Murthy wrote recently in the Harvard Business Review,

> The world is suffering from an epidemic of loneliness. . . . We live in the most technologically connected age in the history of civilization, yet rates of loneliness have doubled since the 1980s. Today, over 40% of adults in America report feeling lonely, and research suggests that the real number may well be higher. . . . And that can be a serious problem. Loneliness and weak social connections are associated with a reduction in lifespan similar to that caused by smoking 15 cigarettes a day . . . At work, loneliness reduces task performance, limits creativity, and impairs other aspects of executive function such as reasoning and decision making.[1]

Paul lays out two fundamental aspects of true, biblical, authentic community, which alone can lift people out of the lonely pseudocommunity of mere connectivity.

The first is *true friendship*, a beautiful and highly coveted relationship that is harder to attain than most people initially imagine. We human beings are so different and diverse in personality and temperament and family and cultural experiences that creating true friendships inevitably involves sporadic bouts of messiness and aggravation. Paul lays out four basic character qualities essential to overcoming these barriers to true friendship: "As a prisoner for the Lord, then, I urge you to live a life worthy of the calling you have received. Be completely humble and gentle; be patient, bearing with one another in love" (Eph. 4:1–2). To bond as true friends, it's important for us to stay the course in learning each other's stories, understanding each other's pain, and accepting one another's foibles. Paul says that can only be accomplished as broken, aggravated (and aggravating!) sinners by striving together for humility and gentleness, patience and forbearance. Hence Gary Thomas tells the stark truth. "The main problem when talking about corporate experience is that in the abstract it's inviting, while in reality it's frustrating. In theory, a group of people committed to sharing Christ together sounds like heaven; in practice, whenever you put a group of people together, you're going to face frustration, sin, and conflict."[2]

We should never allow our differences and diversities to drive us apart, but rather, together, because realizing how alike we are in our differences is the glue of true community. I love how that insight plays out in the 2002 movie *My Big Fat Greek Wedding* in which Nia Vardalos plays Toula Portokalos, the awkward middle child of a proud Greek family. Her father Gus embarrasses her because he always lectures people on Greek history. "Give me a word," he says, "any word, and I'll show you how the root of that word is Greek." Toula meets Ian Miller, a long-haired American teacher, and they fall in love. Her father is livid that she's dating a non-Greek and resists their wedding until, over time, he stops focusing on their differences and beholds instead the sameness of everyone afflicted with the human condition. At the wedding reception, Gus lays out a profound truth about the unity of all human beings (albeit with some sketchy etymology). "Welcome to the Portokalos and to the Miller family. I was thinking last night, the night before my daughter is going to marry Ian Miller, that—you know—the root of the word Miller is a Greek word. Miller comes from the Greek word *milo*, which means 'apple.' So there you go. As many of you know, our name, Portokalos, comes from the Greek word *portokali*, which mean 'orange.' So, here tonight, we have apples and oranges. We are all different. But, in the end, we are all fruit."

Moving as broken people toward community with others who are broken definitely makes us vulnerable to pain, but C. S. Lewis assures us that the risk is worth it. "To love at all is to be vulnerable. Love anything, and your heart will certainly be wrung and possibly be broken. . . . The only place outside Heaven where you can be perfectly safe from all the dangers . . . of love is Hell."[3] Acting in love is always worth risking our safety because after all, "we are all fruit," and the reward is true community. We must always remember that such community is not ultimately about our coddling and comfort, but about being transformed as People of the Book to be better together.

The second aspect of true community that Paul lays out is *spiritual focus*. Mother Teresa once famously noted, "The greatest disease in the West today is not . . . only a poverty of loneliness but also of spirituality. There's a hunger for love, as there is a hunger for God."[4] That's why Paul makes spiritual focus such a priority for People of the Book: "Let the word of Christ dwell in you richly, teaching and admonishing one another in all wisdom, singing psalms and hymns and spiritual songs, with thankfulness in your hearts to God" (Col. 3:16 ESV). He knew that the longevity and depth of any community is a function of its organizing principle. If that principle is, say, fantasy football, then the "community" will last just one season in the league with minimal benefit. True formational Christian community is always based on focused effort applied to understanding and applying the Word of God to our lives.

On June 17, 2015, a small group of mostly African American Christ followers were gathered in Charleston at the Emanuel African Methodist Episcopal Church for Bible study and prayer. A self-styled white supremacist stood up toward the end of the meeting and shot nine worshipers dead. That the survivors and their families were People of the Book who

> **True formational Christian community is always based on focused effort applied to understanding and applying the Word of God to our lives.**

had both "grown and thrived" together was proven days later when they confronted the killer who had murdered their loved ones face to face at the courthouse. The watching world totally expected these Christ followers to vent mightily. But we were all shocked when they chose instead the way of love, as represented by Anthony Thompson. "I forgive you and my family forgives you, but we would like you to take this opportunity to repent . . . confess, give your life to the one who matters the most, Christ, so that He can change it—can change your ways no matter what happened to you, and you will be okay. Do that and you will be better." One by one, these People of the Book rejected the way of power for the way of love, forgiveness, and prayer. The granddaughter of Daniel Simmons Sr. said, "Although my grandfather and the other victims died at the hands of hate, this is proof—everyone's plea for your soul is proof that they lived in love and their legacies will live in love. So, hate won't win . . ." The daughter of Ethel Lance, also killed in the shooting, said to the shooter: "I forgive you. You took something very precious away from me. I will never talk to her ever again. I will never be able to hold her again. But I forgive you, and have mercy on your soul. You hurt me. You hurt a lot of people. But God forgives you, and I forgive you."

In a *Wall Street Journal* article, Peggy Noonan describes what it was like for her to watch and hear the words of these amazing People of the Book: "As I watched I felt I was witnessing something miraculous. I think I did. It was people looking into the eyes of evil, into the eyes of the sick and ignorant shooter who'd blasted a hole in their families, and explaining to him with the utmost forbearance that there is a better way. . . . From the beginning they handled the tragedy with such heart and love. They handled it like a community, a real, alive one that people live within connected to each other."[5] They handled it like a true community for the simple reason that they *were* a true community, better together, and proving Elton Trueblood's observation that "Close contact with a redeemed people makes us both weep and shout for joy, and do both at the same time."[6] True community like we saw in those "better together" Christ followers in Charleston is so wonderful to behold that it fairly breaks hearts with pure joy.

Together We're Stronger

Undoubtedly, true community among Christ followers also makes us *stronger* together. I believe it's a rare human being who doesn't know from personal experience that the opposite of acceptance into community is the debilitating sting of rejection due to the inevitable idiosyncrasies, deficiencies, or perceived handicaps that we all carry. From childhood, when we couldn't ride the tilt-a-whirl at the state fair because we weren't tall enough, to the time we were refused admission because our grades didn't cut it or we were kept out of the club because we weren't cool enough to belong, virtually every one of us has experienced the disheartening bludgeon of rejection. Our differences become, not marks of distinction or potentially unique contributions, but courage-sapping disappointments.

That's how the late actor/comedian Jerry Lewis's character felt in the classic 1957 movie *The Delicate Delinquent*. He played a bumbling janitor named Sidney Pythias who, having failed to gain acceptance by being good, decided to try for acceptance by being bad. He fails even at that, and says to his friend: "When I try to be bad, I'm good. When I try to be good, I'm bad. When I was a kid, I was a jerk. When I was a teenager, I was stupid. Now I'm a man and I'm empty. I know two things about me. One: I'm nothing. And two: I want to be something."

The church community is the one place where discouraged people beaten down into nothing by the world should find the acceptance and encouragement needed to become something beautiful in the world.

As Paul writes, the church community is the one place where discouraged people beaten down into nothing by the world should find the acceptance and encouragement needed to become something beautiful in the world. "May the God who gives endurance and encouragement give you the same attitude of mind toward each other that Christ Jesus had, so that with one mind and one voice you may glorify the God and Father of our Lord Jesus Christ. Accept one another, then, just as Christ accepted you, in order to bring praise to God" (Rom. 15:5–7).

That's exactly what a rather diverse group of men did, according to Samuel in the Old Testament. His almost casual recounting

of the community of David's mighty warriors indicates how they
became stronger together:

> During harvest time, three of the thirty chief warriors came
> down to David at the cave of Adullam, while . . . the Philistine
> garrison was at Bethlehem. David longed for water and said,
> "Oh, that someone would get me a drink of water from the
> well near the gate of Bethlehem!" So the three mighty war-
> riors broke through the Philistine lines, drew water from the
> well near the gate of Bethlehem and carried it back to David.
> (2 Sam. 23:13–16)

Samuel then lists a couple of specific exploits of two members
of "the mighty three," which are both simultaneously random and
wonderful. "Abishai . . . raised his spear against three hundred
men, whom he killed . . . Benaiah son of Jehoiada, a valiant fighter
. . . went down into a pit on a snowy day and killed a lion. And he
struck down a huge Egyptian" (2 Sam. 23:18–21). Samuel's clear
implication in bundling these exploits of David's mighty men is
that alone they were strong, but together they were strongest.

So was a small group of guys in our church who have come
to be called "Benny's Band of Brothers." In April 2015, Benny, a
school facility supervisor, was driving home when he was hit by
a street-racer who ran a stop sign. Benny would spend the next
month in ICU, two weeks on a ventilator. Tough stuff, and all the
more reason it was a blessing that Benny was part of an IBC First
Watch men's small group. These guys met early Friday mornings
to study the Bible and do life in community. The next day, Daniel,
a friend at Benny's First Watch table group, sent out an emergency
email to the rest of the guys—Benny was fighting for his life, and
it was time to step up. After receiving the email, Jason, Daniel,

Grayson, Chris, Greg, Patrick, David, Rich, and Christian started showing up for the long haul at the hospital ICU, the rehab center, and within the wide radius of Benny's wounded life.

The ways they ministered? Meals, for starters. And not just for Benny and his brave wife, Renee, but also for Benny's seven brothers and sisters, who would also be up at the hospital at any given time—up to fifteen people per day. Sometimes the guys went together to deliver meals, like Rich and Jason, who went one day and found Renee particularly moved. She looked at them and said, "Men don't act like this. You blow me away. You wouldn't expect men to take care of us like this."

But not just meals. Chris and Greg took over the lawn duties at Benny's house, mowing his double lot through the heat of our Texas summer. David had an idea to create a GoFundMe account, which raised $6,650 to help with Benny's medical expenses. "If it wasn't for IBC, Benny and I would have lost our car," says Renee. "I am eternally grateful for the way our small groups walked with us through this difficult journey." Benny himself would agree: "I'm grateful that God led me to these guys at IBC because I was reluctant to come at first. I had never been to a multicultural church, but it couldn't have been a better spot for me. These friendships will last forever."

Benny made slow, steady progress. His table guys marveled at his attitude—and especially his humor—through agonizing physical therapy. "It was the Benny Show," they recall. What did Benny's First Watch guys take away from their time of intense care for their friend? One says, "I've seen how important it is to be part of a group; to surround yourself with brothers." Says another: "It brought more hope into my life. I know if something happened to me, they would be there for me." David, one of the guys' former First Watch table members, had moved and been out of the group for a while. But when he heard what had happened, he came back to help. Shortly thereafter, David got married and soon discovered his new wife had breast cancer. But his recent reconnection to his First Watch buddies provided a ready-made stream of support for his new wife and himself. Unbeknownst to him, he had been paving the way for his own comfort when he'd need it most. And then there was fair-haired Christian, a believer from Sion, Switzerland, with a heavy Swiss accent, who went up to the hospital to visit (African American) Benny one day, when the nurse stopped him and said only family members were allowed in ICU. Without missing a beat, and perhaps with the slightest bit of flair, Christian declared, "But I'm his *brother!*" The nurse laughed and let him into the room.[7]

True community as People of the Book makes any motley crew of Christians stronger together whether they find themselves in dungeons, classrooms, break rooms, jails, or hospital intensive care units.

It's obvious that Benny drew strength from the community of his brothers during that long hospital recovery. I hope it's also obvious that Benny's community of brothers themselves drew strength from being together. That fact answers and illustrates Gary Thomas's question, "Why is community worth the bother? Why is such love necessary, as painful as it is? . . . The message of the early church is that simple people could be amazingly powerful when they were members of one another."[8] True community as People of the Book makes any motley crew of Christians stronger together whether they find themselves in dungeons, classrooms, break rooms, jails, or hospital intensive care units. And not just stronger together, but amazingly powerful. Yes, community is most definitely worth the bother!

Together We're Braver

Former US Surgeon General Dr. Vivek H. Murthy told us that loneliness is epidemic in the world. So, unfortunately, is anxiety. In a recent *New York Times Magazine* article, Benoit Denizet-Lewis writes, "Anxiety is the most common mental-health disorder in the United States, affecting nearly one-third of both adolescents and adults, according to the National Institute of Mental Health." He then tells a true story about how anxiety impacted one young man.

> The disintegration of Jake's life . . . happened . . . while he was taking three Advanced Placement classes, running on his school's cross-country team and traveling to Model United Nations conferences. It was a lot to handle, but Jake—the likable, hard-working oldest sibling in a suburban North Carolina family—was the kind of teenager who . . . never really failed at anything . . . so nothing prepared them for the day two years ago when Jake, then 17 . . . refused to go to school and curled up in the fetal position on the floor. "I just can't take it!" he screamed . . . A few weeks later, Jake locked himself in a bathroom at home and tried to drown himself in the bathtub. "It was the depth of hell," his mother said.[9]

Combine loneliness and anxiety long enough in a person's life and it's no surprise when they sink into a hellish sense of perpetual, paralyzed fearfulness. Not every lonely, anxious person suffers as deeply as Jake, but they do suffer with him until reminded of

God's prescription for walking in the way to brave—joining the People of the Book. Remember?

> Be strong and very courageous. Be careful to obey all the law my servant Moses gave you; do not turn from it to the right or to the left, that you may be successful wherever you go. Keep this Book of the Law always on your lips; meditate on it day and night, so that you may be careful to do everything written in it. Then you will be prosperous and successful. Have I not commanded you? Be strong and courageous. Do not be afraid; do not be discouraged, for the LORD your God will be with you wherever you go. (Josh. 1:7–9)

God unmistakably connects strength and courage with diligent training in and application of the Word of God within the context and community of God's people. His promise is that People of the Book are not only better together and stronger together, but braver together as well.

In the New Testament, I believe Paul and his merry band of brothers' exploits in Acts 16 prove Joshua's point. For preaching the gospel and helping people in Philippi, Paul and Silas were stripped, flogged, and thrown into a pitch-black dark dungeon with only the stench of human refuse, the pain of their wounds, and the agony of their feet in stocks for company. But at least they were together. They could draw encouragement from each other. That explains the incredible scene that Dr. Luke describes: "About midnight Paul and Silas were praying and singing hymns to God, and the other prisoners were listening to them" (Acts 16:25).

There's a federal prison in New York called Sing Sing, which was probably not named from Acts 16 (though it should have been)! The word "praying" includes the aspect of praise. Paul and Silas were not raising desperate wails for deliverance, but rather singing heartfelt praise choruses. I imagine in that terrible circumstance I'd be singing, "Rescue the perishing, care for the dying!" But they were singing, "How great thou art!" So with their backs bloody, Paul and Silas together turned the prison blues into jailhouse rock through faith and trust in God. Their backs still screamed with pain, but having a friend along in dire straits makes them less dire. Paul and Silas were undoubtedly braver together.

So were those thirty-three Chilean miners famously rescued from the San José Mine collapse on October 13, 2010, after a record-setting sixty-nine days. Initially they were seventeen days in darkness—the first five of which they could barely breathe from the dust. They stretched a forty-eight-hour emergency food supply into two and a half weeks, rationing tiny sips of milk and two bites of tuna per man every other day. When rescuers finally broke through to them a half-mile underground in unrelenting 90-degree heat with a borehole that brought air and water and food, they also received the news that it could be four months before a rescue shaft could be completed.

Isn't that group of Chilean mine workers a picture of the People of the Book? People trapped in darkness but reached with light and hope from above? People trying to love and care for each other in a difficult place until they get to go together to a better place?

How did they endure? By intentionally forming a beloved community. "'Settling in for the long wait, they have established a disciplined routine designed not only to keep them mentally and physically fit, but working together,' according to the rescue effort's lead psychiatrist, Alberto Benavides. Though some miners requested them, personal music players with headphones were ruled out, because those tend to isolate people from one another. 'What they need is to be together . . . The men know their survival ultimately depends on each other. So in addition to twice-daily prayer sessions, they meet to discuss disagreements, plans and achievements.'"[10]

If you boil it all down, isn't that group of Chilean mine workers a picture of the People of the Book? People trapped in darkness but reached with light and hope from above? People trying to love and care for each other in a difficult place until they get to go together to a better place?

Here's the lesson for us all from the San José mine: "What they need is to be together . . . The men know their survival ultimately depends on each other." We are always better together, stronger together, and braver together. As Elton Trueblood writes, "The renewal of the church will be in progress when it is seen as a fellowship of consciously inadequate persons who gather because they are weak, and to serve because their unity with one another and with Christ has made them bold."[11]

I know from personal experience the boldness granted by community with the People of the Book. I know we are braver together. In another book,[12] I share my experience of fighting for my life against stage IV cancer and how it was the People of the Book (my church community at IBC) that I credit for keeping me on the way to brave. In a letter to our congregation on August 19, 2009, I wrote:

So the IBC staff gets me this pager and puts the number out on the website and in weekend services for people to call when they pray for me . . . I've had that pager on my person now for 5 days. Around the clock, it never stops buzzing. I've found that I can get a passably good massage by holding it at various angles to my neck and shoulders. Sometimes multiple people call simultaneously, producing extra-long buzzes. It's better than the spa. Who needs a masseuse when you can have God's people interceding for you? My doctors wonder why I'm doing so well after major surgery. Guess I should tell them about the pager, eh? All of that to say how grateful I am to you all for your heartfelt prayers, your encouragement through notes and letters and cards and small remembrances which have so powerfully encouraged me and my family in these days. The Lord knows I never actually volunteered to get cancer, but if this is what it took to afford me a personal glimpse into the incredibly encouraging hearts of God's praying people, then I'm grateful even for the disease. Through it, God is showing by you all the true depth of His loving and noble heart in ways I could have previously only imagined.

I was so lifted into the way of brave by my community of Christians that I do believe I would have gone down into a pit on a snowy day and killed a lion. Problem was, I live in Texas, where pits, lions, and snowy days are rare. So instead, through the encouragement of the better/stronger/braver together People of the Book, I just stayed the course in trusting God through my day-to-day journey in the valley of cancer and rejoice that I'm still here today to write these words.

EPILOGUE

The LORD is my light and my salvation—whom shall I fear? The LORD is the stronghold of my life—of whom shall I be afraid? —PSALM 27:1

There is no fear in love. But perfect love drives out fear, because fear has to do with punishment. The one who fears is not made perfect in love. —1 JOHN 4:18

In chapter 1, I wrote about the "Cellist of Sarajevo." I'll end by writing about the "Violinist of Jerusalem." The venue was the Jerusalem Theater in Israel on February 23, 1991. The Persian Gulf War was heating up, and world-famous violinist Isaac Stern had flown from the United States to show support for the Jewish state being threatened by Saddam Hussein's Iraq. At 6:47 p.m., thirteen minutes before the February 23 deadline set by the US for Iraq's withdrawal from Kuwait, sirens sounded over Jerusalem, signaling a Scud missile attack. Inside the sold-out 800-seat Sherover Theater, the ominous wailing clashed with the Mozart concerto being performed by the Israel Philharmonic and featuring the renowned Isaac Stern. The orchestra immediately left the stage, but the audience, prepped beforehand to expect an attack from Iraq, remained and donned their gas masks. During this chaos, Stern stood calmly in place. He chose not to put on a gas mask. Instead, he just launched into Bach's haunting D minor Partita No. 2 for solo violin. He became an intrepid place-maker of peace in a fearful and violent time. Michelle Malkin adds her commentary to this iconic story about an inspiringly courageous man whose faith literally stood up: "Stern once told CNN's Larry King, 'When you believe in something, you can move mountains.' And thwart monsters. Stern's lifelong example of eternal optimism and determined civility in the face of evil should inspire us all. We cannot let our enemies conquer us and cow us into fearful submission. Embrace life. Promote freedom. Celebrate beauty. And resolve—bravely, stubbornly and cheerfully—to play on."[1]

That's what a young shepherd lad named David did long ago when confronting a giant in the Valley of Elah. Strengthened by God's calling, anointing, breaking, testing, and training, David bravely, stubbornly, and cheerfully played on: "Even though I walk through the valley of the shadow of death, I will fear no evil, for you are with me; your rod and your staff, they comfort me" (Ps. 23:4 ESV). Why did David fear no evil in the battle against Goliath? Simply this. Like Isaac Stern almost three thousand years later, he *believed in something*—the presence and power and love of God in his life. "I'm not afraid, Lord, because you are *here!*" David knew that God was with him because God had called him to a specific mission, and David said yes. David knew that God was with him because God had anointed him with the Holy Spirit and broken his pride and tested his faith and trained him skillfully. "Lord, you are *here!*"

Of course, the giants we Christians face today and our God-given mission with respect to facing those giants differs from David's mission to slay Goliath long ago. But though we have a different mission from God as Christians in the modern world, we still live with a deep need for courage in a fearful land of giants. Max Lucado describes our continuing dilemma:

> Each sunrise seems to bring fresh reasons for fear. They're talking layoffs at work, slowdowns in the economy, flare-ups in the Middle East, turnovers at headquarters, downturns in

the housing market, upswings in global warming. . . . The plague of our day, terrorism, begins with the word *terror*. . . . Fear, it seems, has taken up a hundred-year lease on the building next door and set up shop. . . . Fear herds us into a prison and slams the doors. Wouldn't it be great to walk out?"[2]

I'd only add the increasing secularization of American culture and the resulting loss of Christian religious freedom to Max's list of intimidating developments.

And so the spiritual battle rages and will continue to rage. Giants remain in the valley today, menacing giants that block our way when we want to go with God, malicious giants that wage war upon us when we determine to live for Christ.

Therefore I do enthusiastically affirm with Max that it would be so great "to walk out," and I declare that we can indeed do so if only we will take the way to brave. If only we will walk in the faithful, long-suffering, and diligent path that Christian disciples have followed for mil-

We will be tried, trained, and true believers who strategically know and humbly pursue God's calling in the power of His Holy Spirit, who has repeatedly defanged serpents and shrunk giants to size. But we must do all this not as lone rangers, but as friends and family together in the body of Christ.

lennia, then God will shape in us a "David faith" for our Goliath world. If we will only embrace being *called* and *anointed* and *broken* and *tested* and *trained* as dust-covered Christ followers, we will be unflappably courageous, not increasingly fearful in the storm but deeply intrepid through the storm. We will be tried, trained, and true believers who strategically know and humbly pursue God's calling in the power of His Holy Spirit, who has repeatedly defanged serpents and shrunk giants to size. But we must do all this not as lone rangers, but as friends and family together in the body of Christ.

Remember how Peter and John demonstrated the proven effect of a united community of faith early in the book of Acts: "Then Peter, filled with the Holy Spirit, said to them . . . 'Salvation is found in no one else, for there is no other name under heaven given to mankind by which we must be saved.' When they saw the courage of Peter and John and realized that they were unschooled, ordinary men, they were astonished and they took note that these men had been with Jesus" (Acts 4:8, 12–13). Courage was the singular quality of the apostles most noted by an adversarial power structure as evidence that the apostles were part of that unique community that had been with Jesus. It was not any certified character education, but their time with Jesus that had transformed them from being mere bungling knuckleheads into purpose-driven representatives of the Lord of the universe. Jesus will do this same thing for us Christ followers too, in and through our communities of faith, as our churches get back to the New Testament cultivation of faithful discipleship.

It was not any certified character education, but their time with Jesus that had transformed them from being mere bungling knuckleheads into purpose-driven representatives of the Lord of the universe.

As I wrote at the outset of this book, and then specifically in chapter 10, courage is not a virtue that can be sought in isolation. Rather, it's a serendipity, a bonus benefit that we receive in the package deal of love-induced discipleship focused on bearing one another's burdens and, as the church, being *with* God *for* blessing the world around us. As Tod Bolsinger observes:

> Christian community is not merely about connection, care and belonging. Spiritual transformation is not just about becoming more like Christ as an end in itself. In a post-Christendom world that has become a mission field right outside the sanctuary door, Christian community is about gathering and forming a people, and spiritual transformation is about both individual and corporate growth, so that they—together—participate in Christ's mission to establish the kingdom of God "on earth as it is in heaven."[3]

Because Christian community *is* the place where God gathers and forms a people and shapes a David faith in them, the flourishing of Christ-centered churches is of the utmost importance! It is in these churches that believers *together* can participate bravely in Christ's mission to establish the kingdom of God "on earth as it is in heaven," because it is in these churches that courage will become contagious. Hang around Isaac Stern in Jerusalem, and you'll catch it. Hang around David in Elah, and you'll catch it. Hang around Peter in Jerusalem, and you'll catch it. Hang around Jesus, and you'll catch it! It was not SEAL training but their time with Jesus and each other that transformed the apostles into courageous ambassadors of the Lord.

Our time with Jesus and each other in the body of Christ will do the same for us in our land of giants. As Brett McCracken writes, "Good faith endures not because it is trendy but because it is transcendent; not because it is old, but because it is eternal. We may be in a Babylon-like culture, but we are citizens of the City of

God, 'a city with foundations, whose architect and builder is God' (Heb. 11:10). For that reason we needn't freak out, but rather press on in our Eden-old task: to image the Creator by ordering a chaotic world, keeping the light alive amidst a formidable darkness."[4]

Yes, we still live in a land of giants. But Brett is right—we needn't freak out! All we need do is be covered by the dust of our Master, for as we learn to trust Him more, we can fear giants less. "The steadfast of mind You will keep in perfect peace, because he trusts in You . . . GOD the LORD, we have an everlasting Rock" (Isaiah 26:3–4 NASB). And if we follow harder after Jesus, we can worry less. "Peace I leave with you; my peace I give you. I do not give to you as the world gives. Do not let your hearts be troubled and do not be afraid" (John 14:27). And if we let the Lord lead us and fill us and break us and test us and train us, we can stress less. "For the Spirit God gave us does not make us timid, but gives us power, love and self-discipline" (2 Tim. 1:7). We can walk fear-free in a world where beautiful and terrible things continue to happen because we have a powerfully constructed faith of the lamp-lighting, darkness-illuminating, troop-running, wall-leaping, people-shielding (and giant-slaying!) variety (see Psalm 18).

Being covered by the dust of our Master doesn't mean we'll never get scared. It means we will never fear as a way of life, but rather we will be intrepid believers who do not know the unknown future but trust the One who does. Who are not weak in their aloneness but made strong by Him who is a very present help in trouble. Who do not worry, but trust. Who do not dread, but pray. Who do not freak out, but move in. Who are not bulletproof, but walk in peace.

My friends, what giants do you face in these momentous days? Where is your Valley of Elah? Please claim David's battle-cry as your own: *for the battle is the LORD's, and he will give all of you into our hands.* You don't need more knowledge, faith, or time to do what you know God wants you to do. You just need courage. And God has given it to you through Christ! David, Jesus, Peter, and John got off the sidelines and proved their courage by doing the right thing whatever it took, whatever the cost, so that God's will was done on the earth for His glory and the good of His people. Will we likewise walk in the way of brave? Will we resolve—bravely, stubbornly, and cheerfully—to play on? We will if we get off the sidelines, step into the valley, and follow our giant-slayer of old by declaring with David, "The Lord is my light and my salvation—whom shall I fear? The Lord is the stronghold of my life—of whom shall I be afraid?" (Ps. 27:1).

Of whom indeed?

NOTES

Introduction: Beautiful and Terrible Things Will Happen

1. Frederick Buechner, *Beyond Words: Daily Readings in the ABC's of Faith* (New York: HarperOne, 2004), 139.

2. At issue was a blog post Vought had written as an alumnus of Wheaton College (that's my Alma Mater, just saying!) in response to a controversy involving one of its faculty members. The offending passage was this: "Muslims do not simply have a deficient theology. They do not know God because they have rejected Jesus Christ his Son, and they stand condemned." While it may sound harsh to a non-Christian, Vought was in no way suggesting that Muslims cannot be good citizens or should be treated severely by the governing authorities. He was simply reiterating what the vast majority of Christians have believed for two millennia: that Jesus is the way, the truth, and the life, and that no one comes to the Father except through Him (John 14:7).

3. As a Texas pastor, I felt my Houston colleagues' pain just a few years ago when that city's mayor subpoenaed their sermons in advance for political correctness vetting. See Josh Sanburn, "Houston's Pastors Outraged After City Subpoenas Sermons Over Transgender Bill," *Time*, October 17, 2014, http://time.com/3514166/houston-pastors-sermons-subpoenaed/.

4. The Washington State Supreme Court effectively put seventy-two-year-old grandmother Barronelle Stutzman out of business by fining her hundreds of thousands of dollars for declining to create custom floral arrangements for longtime customer and friend Rob Ingersoll's same-sex wedding. Even though he sought to bankrupt her, she continues to love and wish him the best to this very day. See Jim Campbell, "Barronelle Stutzman Shows Sexual Orientation Laws Treat Religious People Like Racists," *The Federalist*, February 27, 2017, http://thefederalist.com/2017/02/27/barronelle-stutzman-shows-sexual-orientation-laws-treat-religious-people-like-racists/.

5. In the battleground between LGBTQ protections and free exercise protections for religious businesses and institutions, last year California debated a law (SB 1146) that would have subjected Christian colleges and universities to lawsuits and loss of state financial aid for their students if they continued enforcing admissions, housing, hiring, and other policies based on their traditional beliefs about sexuality and gender. Though SB 1146 was (thankfully) amended to remove its most controversial parts, for Christian colleges across America it was an ominous sign of things to come, even though met with a collective shrug by mainstream American culture. "Never mind that universities were invented by Christians . . . Christians are discriminatory, dumb, and dangerous, and society is better off without them." Ironically, that was the same message received by Little Sisters of the Poor when, under the Affordable Care Act, the US government sued these humble (yet apparently "discriminatory, dumb, and dangerous") Catholic nuns for not including abortion coverage in their group health insurance plan! See Brett McCracken, "Fearless Faith in a Time of Forgetting," *Christianity Today*, August 30, 2016, http://www.christianitytoday.com/ct/2016/august-web-only/fearless-faith-in-time-of-forgetting.html.

6. After I publicly challenged the huge abortion boost contained in the original Affordable Care Act in a sermon, I was threatened with the Johnson Rule (which allows a church to be stripped of its tax-exempt status for engaging in what the IRS deems "political activity"). See Kinsey Hasstedt, "Abortion Coverage Under the Affordable Care Act: Advancing Transparency, Ensuring Choice and Facilitating Access," *Guttmacher Policy Review* 18, no. 1 (April 2015), https://www.guttmacher.org/gpr/2015/04/abortion-coverage-under-affordable-care-act-advancing-transparency-ensuring-choice-and.
7. Peter Mommsen, "A Time for Courage," *Plough Quarterly*, Issue 12, Spring 2017, https://www.plough.com/en/topics/faith/discipleship/a-time-for-courage.
8. Quoted by Peter Mommsen, ibid.
9. John Bright, *A History of Israel*, 2nd ed. (Philadelphia: Westminster Press, 1972), 186.

SECTION 1: GOD CALLS US
1. Cian Power, "Kingship in the Hebrew Bible," Teaching the Bible, Society of Biblical Literature e-newsletter, https://www.sbl-site.org/assets/pdfs/TBv3i3_Power Kingship.pdf.
2. George Bernard Shaw and Stanley Weintraub, *Man and Superman: A Comedy and a Philosophy*, ed. Dan H. Laurence (1903; repr. New York: Penguin Classics, 2001).

Chapter 1: Gardens, Not Walls
Epigraph #1: St. Francis of Assisi: Robert J. Spitzer, *Five Pillars of the Spiritual Life: A Practical Guide to Prayer for Active People* (San Francisco: Ignatius Press, 2008), 60.
1. This is Dr. Barry Jones's descriptive phrase; see below in *Dwell*, 53.
2. Strong's Concordance 7965.
3. Saint Augustine, *Confessions*, trans. R. S. Pine-Coffin (New York: Penguin, 1961), 21.
4. Barry D. Jones and Michael Frost, *Dwell: Life with God for the World* (Downers Grove, IL: IVP Books, 2014), 53.
5. Connie Cass, "In God We Trust, Maybe, but Not Each Other," Associated Press, November 30, 2013, http://ap-gfkpoll.com/featured/our-latest-poll-findings-24; quoted in Eric Metaxas, "Angry America," BreakPoint, December 10, 2013, http://www.breakpoint.org/2013/12/angry-america/.
6. Ray Pritchard, "God's Peace Corps" (sermon), Keep Believing Ministries, March 3, 1996, https://www.keepbelieving.com/sermon/1996-03-03-gods-peace-corps/.
7. Walter C. Kaiser, Jr., "Israel's Missionary Call," in *Perspectives on the World Christian Movement* (Pasadena, CA: William Carey Library, 2009), 28.
8. Cornelius Plantinga, Jr., *Not the Way It's Supposed to Be: A Breviary of Sin* (Grand Rapids: Eerdmans, 1996), 14.
9. Simon Carey Holt, *God Next Door: Spirituality and Mission in the Neighbourhood* (Victoria, Australia: Acorn Press, Limited, 2007), 28.
10. N. T. Wright, *Simply Christian: Why Christianity Makes Sense* (New York: HarperOne, 2010), 236.
11. Andy Crouch, "The Myth of Engaging the Culture," *Christianity Today*, July/August 2016, 33.

12. Scott McClellan wrote Jesse's story in "Healing Tables," IBC eLetter, July 5, 2017, http://www.irvingbible.org/blog/07-05-2017/healing-tables.

Chapter 2: Servant Exiles

1. Jim Reeves, "This World is Not My Home," Sony/ATV Music Publishing.
2. Richard John Neuhaus, *American Babylon: Notes of a Christian Exile* (New York: Basic Books, 2009), 32.
3. Bryan Stone, quoted in Barry D. Jones and Michael Frost, *Dwell: Life with God for the World* (Downers Grove, IL: IVP Books, 2014), 198.
4. International Movie Database, http://www.imdb.com/title/tt0124879/quotes.
5. David Kinnaman and Gabe Lyons, *Good Faith: Being a Christian When Society Thinks You're Irrelevant and Extreme* (Grand Rapids: Baker Books, 2016), 75–76.
6. Richard Peace, *Holy Conversation: Talking About God in Everyday Life* (Downers Grove, IL: InterVarsity Press, 2006), 58.
7. Tacitus, *Annales* xv. 44; *Documents of the Christian Church*, Henry Bettenson and Chris Maunder, eds. (Oxford: Oxford University Press, 2011), 2.
8. Charles E. Moore, "Pandemic Love," Plough, https://www.plough.com/en/topics/faith/discipleship/pandemic-love.
9. David Brooks, "The Next Culture War," *New York Times*, June 30, 2015, https://www.nytimes.com/2015/06/30/opinion/david-brooks-the-next-culture-war.html.
10. Water is Basic is a borehole drilling organization in the Republic of South Sudan birthed in 2006 and led by Sudanese religious leaders, in conjunction with Irving Bible Church, with one goal: to provide clean water as quickly as possible to as many people as possible. We finished our first well in 2008 and since then have installed five hundred and restored seventy-five more. Total investment has grown to over $5 million for equipment, local salaries, training, and supplies. Water is Basic was formed as a U.S. 501(c)(3) organization in 2012 to support these efforts in South Sudan.
11. Brooks, "The Next Culture War."
12. Charles J. Chaput, *Strangers in a Strange Land: Living the Catholic Faith in a Post-Christian World* (New York: Henry Holt and Company, 2017), 1.
13. See Elesha Coffman, "What is the origin of the Christian fish symbol?," *Christian History*, 2008, http://www.christianitytoday.com/history/2008/august/what-is-origin-of-christian-fish-symbol.html.
14. Ibid.
15. Wikipedia's "Constantine the Great and Christianity" entry, https://en.wikipedia.org/wiki/Constantine_the_Great_and_Christianity.
16. Andrew Quinn, "The Hobby Lobby Case Is a Small Victory, But a Real One," *The Federalist*, July 2, 2014, http://thefederalist.com/2014/07/02/the-hobby-lobby-case-is-a-small-victory-but-a-real-one/.
17. Mollie Hemingway, "Media Want To Make Sure You Never Hear About 'The Little Sisters Of The Poor,'" *The Federalist*, May 17, 2016, http://thefederalist.com/2016/05/17/media-want-to-make-sure-you-never-hear-about-the-little-sisters-of-the-poor/.
18. Henri Nouwen, *The Return of the Prodigal Son: A Story of Homecoming* (New York: Doubleday, 1994), 39.
19. Ryan Sanders, *Unbelievable: Examining the Unlikely Beauty of the Christian Story* (Addison, TX: HIS Publishing Group, 2017), 12.

SECTION 2: GOD ANOINTS US
  1. Tertullian, *On Flight in Persecution* 9, cf. 10, 11.

Chapter 3: The Wild Goose
  1. J. R. R. Tolkien, *The Hobbit* (Boston: Houghton Mifflin Harcourt, 2012), 78.
  2. We know that the Holy Spirit is God for many reasons. Divine names are given
     to him (Acts 5:3-4; 1 Cor. 3:16). Also, divine perfections are attributed to Him.
     For example, the Holy Spirit is omnipresent (Ps. 139:7–10), omniscient (Isa.
     40:13–14), omnipotent (1 Cor. 12:11), and eternal (Heb. 9:14). The Holy Spirit
     was involved in creation (Gen. 1:2), the new birth (John 3:5–6), and the resurrec-
     tion of the dead (Rom. 8:11). Finally, divine honor is paid to him (as in the "Great
     Commission" where the Holy Spirit holds the same status as the Father and Son
     (Matt. 28:19; see also Rom. 9:1; 2 Cor. 13:14).
  3. Francis Chan, *Forgotten God: Reversing Our Tragic Neglect of the Holy Spirit*
     (Colorado Springs: David C. Cook, 2009).
  4. Michael S. Horton, "Getting To Know The Shy Member of the Trinity," *I Believe
     In the Holy Spirit*, September 1, 1992.
  5. A. W. Tozer, *A Treasury of A. W. Tozer* (Grand Rapids: Baker Book House, 1980),
     41.
  6. Frederick Buechner, *Telling the Truth: The Gospel as Tragedy, Comedy, and Fairy
     Tale* (San Francisco: HarperSanFrancisco, 1977), 84.
  7. Ray Simpson, *Exploring Celtic Spirituality* (London: Hodder & Stoughton, 1995),
     121.
  8. Personal characteristics are attributed to the Holy Spirit. He has intelligence:
     "When the Advocate comes, whom I will send to you from the Father, the Spirit
     of truth who goes out from the Father, he will testify about me" (John 15:26; see
     also John 14:26; Rom. 8:16). He has emotions: "And do not grieve the Holy Spirit
     of God, with whom you were sealed for the day of redemption" (Eph. 4:30; see
     also Isa. 63:10). And He has a will: "Paul and his companions traveled through-
     out the region of Phrygia and Galatia, having been kept by the Holy Spirit from
     preaching the word in the province of Asia. When they came to the border of
     Mysia, they tried to enter Bithynia, but the Spirit of Jesus would not allow them
     to" (Acts 16:6-7; see also 1 Cor. 12:11). Also, the Holy Spirit does things people
     do, such as speaking, searching, testifying, commanding, revealing, striving, and
     making intercession (cf. Gen. 1:2; 6:3; Luke 12:12; John 14:26; 15:26; 16:8; Acts
     8:29; 13:2; Rom. 8:11; 1 Cor. 2:10, 11).
  9. Ian Coffey, "Deep Impact," Keswick '99, OM Publishing, submitted by Owen
     Bourgaize, Guernsey, United Kingdom, *Preaching Today*, http://www.preaching
     today.com/illustrations/2000/november/12715.html?view=comments.
 10. Gordon Fee, *Paul, the Spirit, and the People of God* (Peabody, MA: Hendrickson,
     1996), 21.
 11. Mark Batterson uses the term "Wild Goose chase" in his book *Wild Goose
     Chase: Reclaim the Adventure of Pursuing God* (Colorado Springs: Multnomah,
     2008).
 12. "Our Catholic Prayers," http://www.ourcatholicprayers.com/st-patricks-
     breastplate.html. "St. Patrick's Breastplate is a popular prayer attributed to one
     of Ireland's most beloved patron saints. According to tradition, St. Patrick wrote
     it in 433 A.D. for divine protection before successfully converting the Irish King
     Leoghaire and his subjects from paganism to Christianity. . . .

More recent scholarship suggests its author was anonymous. In any case, this prayer certainly reflects the spirit with which St. Patrick brought our faith to Ireland! St. Patrick's Breastplate, also known as The Lorica of Saint Patrick was popular enough to inspire a hymn based on this text as well. (This prayer has also been called The Cry of the Deer.)"

13. Chan, *Forgotten God*, 37.
14. Andy McQuitty, *Notes from the Valley: A Spiritual Cancer Travelogue* (Chicago: Moody Publishers, 2015), 15.
15. "I consider the valley here mentioned to be the same as the valley of Bochim, mentioned in Judges 2:1 Judges 2:5, which received its name from the weeping of the Jews, when they were rebuked by an angel for their disobedience to the commands of God" (Charles H. Spurgeon, *The Treasury of David*, 1885, http://www.biblestudytools.com/commentaries/treasury-of-david/psalms-84-6.html).
16. Amanda Cook, "You Make Me Brave," Bethel Music 2014.

Chapter 4: Catch the Wind

Epigraph #1: Tony Jones and Phyllis Tickle, *The Sacred Way: Spiritual Practices for Everyday Life* (Grand Rapids: Zondervan/Youth Specialties, 2005), 26.

Epigraph #2: Ray Pritchard, "Life in the Spirit," June 20, 1993, https://www.keepbelieving.com/sermon/life-in-the-spirit/.

1. Frederick Buechner, *The Longing for Home: Recollections and Reflections* (New York: HarperCollins, 1996), 121.
2. Max Lucado, *The Applause of Heaven* (City: Word Publishing, 1999), 32.
3. Story drawn from Voice of the Martyrs (Persecution Blog, May 24, 2011), and Richard Wurmbrand, *Tortured for Christ*.
4. Karen Hinckley, DJ, #49, p. 45.
5. Jim Cymbala, *Fresh Wind Fresh Fire* (Grand Rapids: Zondervan, 1997), 73.
6. Calvin Miller, *The Path of Celtic Prayer* (Downers Grove, IL: InterVarsity Press, 2007), 17–18.
7. A similar Celtic lorica comes down from the *Carmina Gadelica*, "Uriel shall be at my feet, Ariel shall be at my back, Gabriel shall be at my head, And Raphael shall be at my side." Calvin Miller, ibid., 116.
8. Sara Germano, "Yoga Poseurs: Athletic Gear Soars, Outpacing Sport Itself," *Wall Street Journal*, August 20, 2014, sec. Business, http://www.wsj.com/articles/yoga-poseurs-athletic-apparel-moves-out-of-the-gym-to-every-day-1408561182.
9. In The Message paraphrase of Romans 3–4, we read, "And now what the law code asked for but we couldn't deliver is accomplished as we, instead of redoubling our own efforts, simply embrace what the Spirit is doing in us."

SECTION 3: GOD BREAKS US

1. Jeremy Myers, "Did David's Mother Commit Adultery?," *Redeeming God*, https://redeeminggod.com/davids-mother-commit-adultery/.

Chapter 5: Crucible and Character

Epigraph #1: Quoted in Charles R. Swindoll, *Insights on Romans* (Tyndale House, 2015), 185–86.

1. Eugene H. Peterson, *Practice Resurrection: A Conversation on Growing Up in Christ*, rep. ed. (Wm. B. Eerdmans Publishing Co., 2013).

2. Mark McMinn, *Why Sin Matters: The Surprising Relationship Between Our Sin and God's Grace* (Carol Stream, IL: Tyndale, 2004), 69–71.
3. Jerry Useem, "Power Causes Brain Damage", *Atlantic Monthly*, July/August 2017, 24.
4. Gordon MacDonald, *Ordering Your Private World* (Nashville: Thomas Nelson, 2017), 133.
5. F. B. Meyer, *Israel: A Prince with God; the Story of Jacob Retold* (New York: Revell, 1891), 101.
6. Max Lucado, *God Came Near* (Nashville: Thomas Nelson, 2004), 73.
7. John Eldredge, *Wild at Heart: Discovering the Secret of a Man's Soul*, 3.4.2001 edition (Nashville: Thomas Nelson, 2001), 137.

Chapter 6: The Beautiful Broken

Epigraph #1: Quoted in Charles R. Swindoll, *Come Before Winter and Share My Hope* (Grand Rapids: Zondervan, 1994), 489–91.
1. Vance Havner, *Christian Reader*, Vol. 32, no. 4.
2. Theodore Roder, "His Liberating Touch," *Discipleship Journal* (July/August 1984).
3. John Eldredge, *Waking the Dead: The Secret to a Heart Fully Alive* (Nashville: Nelson Books, 2016), 42.
4. Alan Nelson, "Broken in the Right Place", *Discipleship Journal*, #94.
5. C. S. Lewis, *Mere Christianity* (New York: McMillan Publishing, 1952), 86.
6. Story drawn from Sam Whatley, *Pondering the Journey*.
7. John Eldredge, *Wild at Heart: Discovering the Secret of a Man's Soul* (Nashville: Thomas Nelson, 2001), 52..
8. Walter Anderson, *Courage Is a Three-Letter Word* (Random House, 1986).
9. Brennan Manning, *Abba's Child: The Cry of the Heart for Intimate Belonging* (Colorado Springs: NavPress, 2002), 25.
10. Brené Brown, "The Power of Vulnerability, TEDxHouston, 20:19, Filmed June 2010.
11. Ann Voskamp, *The Broken Way: A Daring Path into the Abundant Life* (Grand Rapids: Zondervan, 2016), 264.
12. Blackie Sherrod, "Words from out of the Past Enlighten and Encourage," *Dallas Morning News*, May 27, 1988, sec. 3B.
13. Alternate beatitudes drawn from Catholic Education Resource Center "Television Statistics and Sources."
14. Clarence Jordan, *Sermon on the Mount* (Judson Press, 1970).
15. Gordon MacDonald, "Transforming Failure," *Discipleship Journal*, Issue 109, 1999, 59.
16. Voskamp, *The Broken Way*, 264.

SECTION 4: GOD TESTS US

Chapter 7: Lions and Tigers and Bears (and Giants), Oh My!

Epigraph #1: Ralph Waldo Emerson, "Culture," in *The Conduct of Life*, 1860.
1. Krish Kandiah, "When God Does the Unexpected," *Christianity Today*, Christianitytoday.com, March 2017, 54.
2. Peach grower: Paul Lee Tan, *Encyclopedia of 7700 Illustrations : A Treasury of Illustrations, Anecdotes, Facts and Quotations for Pastors, Teachers and Christian Workers* (Garland TX: Bible Communications, 1996, c1979).

3. John Ortberg, *The Me I Want to Be: Becoming God's Best Version of You* (Grand Rapids: Zondervan, 2010), 237.

4. George Whitefield, *1001 Quotations That Connect: Timeless Wisdom for Preaching, Teaching, and Writing* (HarperCollins Christian Publishing, 2009), 35.

5. Peter Kennedy, "Devotional - Trials Strengthen Our Faith," Devotional.com, May 3, 2015, http://www.devotional.com/Blog/Devotionals/Devotions-In-Letters-Of-Peter/1438/.

6. Ben Jonson, *The Works of Ben Jonson*, vol. 7th (London: D. Midwinter, 1756), 70.

7. J. I. Packer, *Your Father Loves You: Daily Insights for Knowing God* (Wheaton, IL: Harold Shaw Publishers, 1986), 20.

8. Unknown Confederate soldier, "The Blessing of Unanswered Prayers," http://www.beliefnet.com/prayers/protestant/gratitude/the-blessing-of-unanswered-prayers.aspx.

9. Andrew Murray, quoted by Amy Carmichael, *Though the Mountains Shake* (South India: Dohnavur Fellowship, 1943), 12.

10. William F. Buckley, Jr., "Malcolm Muggeridge and the Longing for Faith," *Washington Post*, November 24, 1990, https://www.washingtonpost.com/archive/opinions/1990/11/24/malcolm-muggeridge-and-the-longing-for-faith/21f8650a-b1e6-4b3c-a396-381b5a4cc1a0/.

11. Jon Bloom, "When God Feels Cruel," *Desiring God*, October 6, 2014, https://www.desiringgod.org/articles/when-god-feels-cruel.

12. Interview by Steve Turner with Steven Curtis Chapman, "Don't Miss Steven Curtis Chapman's Point," *Christianity Today*, February 17, 2017, http://www.christianitytoday.com/ct/2017/march/dont-miss-steven-curtis-chapmans-point.html.

13. Mark Batterson, *In a Pit with a Lion on a Snowy Day: How to Survive and Thrive When Opportunity Roars* (New York: Multnomah, 2006), 18.

Chapter 8: Faith Stands Up

Epigraph #1: https://www.americanswhotellthetruth.org/portraits/jim-hightower.

Epigraph #2: Billy Graham, "A Time for Moral Courage," *Reader's Digest*, July 1964.

1. Interview by Hunter Baker with Mark Sayers, "Why the Modern World Is Making Us Miserable," *Christianity Today*, May 26, 2017, http://www.christianitytoday.com/ct/2017/june/how-bible-helps-us-live-well-in-world-gone-mad.html.

2. David Burchett, at Northeast Bible Church, March 27, 1985. (Today Dave is an Emmy Award–winning television sports director, author, and Christian speaker. He is the author of *When Bad Christians Happen to Good People* and *Bring' em Back Alive: A Healing Plan for Those Wounded by the Church*).

3. Dave Barry, quoted by John Ortberg, *If You Want to Walk on Water, You've Got to Get Out of the Boat* (Zondervan, 2008), 122.

4. Henri J. M. Nouwen, *Our Greatest Gift: A Meditation on Dying and Caring* (New York: HarperCollins, 2009).

5. Jay Nordlinger, "Evan Mawarire: Zimbabwe's Freedom Pastor," July 10, 2017, https://www.nationalreview.com/magazine/2017-07-09-2050/evan-mawarire-zimbabwes-freedom-pastor. ©2017 National Review. Used with permission.

6. This is the author's retelling of 1 Samuel 17:48–51 while taking some artistic liberty.

7. Dietrich Bonhoeffer, *Letters and Papers from Prison* (New York: Touchstone, 1997), 228–29.

SECTION 5: GOD TRAINS US
Chapter 9: Eat This Book

1. Eugene H. Peterson, *Eat This Book: A Conversation in the Art of Spiritual Reading*, (Grand Rapids, Mich.: Eerdmans, 2009).
2. Story closely drawn from William F. Buckley, "How Space Shuttles Got That Way or Why Engineering Is an Exact Science," *National Review*, Jan 24, 2000, 15. ©2017 National Review. Used with permission.
3. Augustine, *Confessions of Saint Augustine*, Book VIII, Chapter 12.
4. *epanorthosis* for those who care . . .
5. Eugene H. Peterson, *Eat This Book: A Conversation in the Art of Spiritual Reading* (Grand Rapids: Eerdmans, 2009).

Chapter 10: The People of the Book

Epigraph #1: Joseph H. Hellerman, *When the Church Was a Family: Recapturing Jesus' Vision for Authentic Christian Community* (Nashville: B&H, 2009), 1.
Epigraph #2: Gary Thomas, *The Beautiful Fight: Surrendering to the Transforming Presence of God Every Day of Your Life* (Grand Rapids: Zondervan, 2007), 217.

1. Vivek H. Murthy, "Work and the Loneliness Epidemic," *Harvard Business Review*, Oct 2017.
2. Gary Thomas, *The Beautiful Fight: Surrendering to the Transforming Presence of God Every Day of Your Life* (Grand Rapids: Zondervan, 2007), 214.
3. C. S. Lewis, *The Four Loves* (New York: Harvest Books, 1971), 169.
4. Mother Teresa, *A Simple Path* (New York: Ballantine Books, 1995).
5. Peggy Noonan, "A Bow to Charleston," *Wall Street Journal*, June 19, 2015, https://blogs.wsj.com/peggynoonan/2015/06/19/a-bow-to-charleston/.
6. Elton Trueblood, *The Incendiary Fellowship* (New York: Harper and Row, 1967), 107.
7. Story context drawn from "Benny's Band of Brothers" by Julie Rhodes, *Chatter Magazine*, September 19, 2016.
8. Thomas, *The Beautiful Fight*, 217.
9. Benoit Denizet-Lewis, "Why Are More American Teenagers Than Ever Suffering From Severe Anxiety?", *The New York Times Magazine*, October 11, 2017, https://www.nytimes.com/2017/10/11/magazine/why-are-more-american-teenagers-than-ever-suffering-from-severe-anxiety.html.
10. Wil Longbottom and Graham Gurrin, "'That was a long shift': Foreman is the last of the 33 trapped Chilean miners to be delivered to freedom," *Daily Mail*, October 14, 2010, http://www.dailymail.co.uk/news/article-1320045/CHILEAN-MINERS-RESCUE-Back-dead-69-days-trapped-underground.html.
11. Trueblood, *The Incendiary Fellowship*, 107.
12. Andy McQuitty, *Notes from the Valley: A Spiritual Travelogue through Cancer* (Chicago: Moody Publishers, 2015).

Epilogue

1. Michelle Malkin, "Isaac Stern's Inspiration, *Washington Times*, September 30, 2001, http://www.washingtontimes.com/news/2001/sep/30/20010930-025649-8873r/.
2. Max Lucado, *Fearless: Imagine Your Life Without Fear* (Nashville: Thomas Nelson, 2012), 4–5.

3. Tod Bolsinger, *Canoeing the Mountains: Christian Leadership in Uncharted Territory* (Downers Grove, IL: IVP Books, 2015), 39.

4. Brett McCracken, "Fearless Faith in a Time of Forgetting," *Christianity Today*, August 30, 2016, http://www.christianitytoday.com/ct/2016/august-web-only/fearless-faith-in-time-of-forgetting.html.

ACKNOWLEDGMENTS

I want to express my appreciation to many friends who contributed to *The Way to Brave*. Thanks to Jeremiah Betron, whose expert editing assistance improved not only the form but also the content of this book and to Donna O'Reilly, my ever-faithful assistant who has for years kept my pastoral train from jumping the tracks. Thanks to John Couch for the use of his wonderful horse barn office in SoCal to write the proposal and to Liz and Beth and Alice McQuitty and Duane Sherman for patiently encouraging me with early ideas in the inception of *The Way to Brave*. Thanks to Allen Arnold, whose professional advice shaped the tone and structure of the book in its earliest form. Thanks to Dr. Barry Jones for his passion for the biblical concept of Shalom (as expressed among other places in the fine book *Dwell*), which informs the first section of the book. Also to IBC Communications pastor Scott McClellan, whose superb writings powerfully shape our church culture, and for pastors David Grant and Jason Stein, whose visionary leadership (along with Scott's) created the IBC discipleship ministry *Foundation*, which greatly influenced section 5 of this book. Finally, thanks to all the pastors, elders and staff, and congregation of Irving Bible Church for being the "cellists of Sarajevo" right here in twenty-first century northeast Texas ... the "place of peace" you created here is the ultimate inspiration for *The Way to Brave*.

A spiritual travelogue through cancer

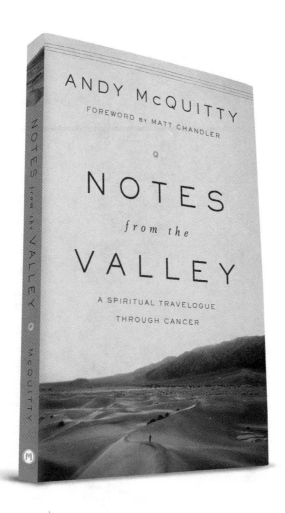

MOODY Publishers

From the Word to Life

Notes from the Valley is Andy McQuitty's travelogue through the desert valley of stage-four cancer. Simultaneously pastoral, evangelistic, theological, and authentic, this book is for anyone on the cancer journey who is craving words of God's wisdom for their journey.

978-0-8024-1254-6 | ALSO AVAILABLE AS AN EBOOK

Learn from the team that established the early church

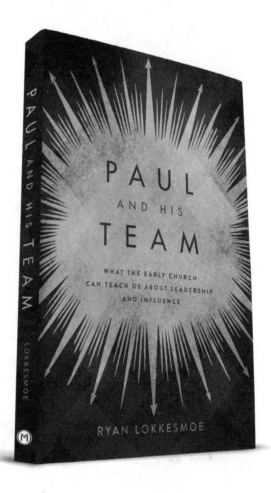

Rethinking success in ministry

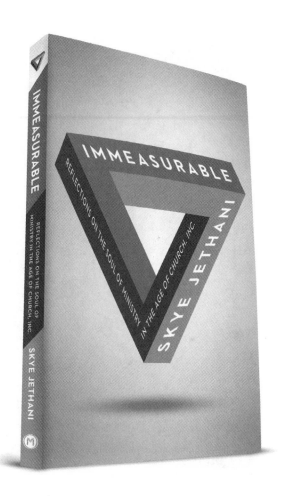

Immeasurable helps ministers recognize the cultural forces shaping their view of the calling, and then reimagine what faithful church leaders can look like in the twenty-first century. Through short essays and reflections on aspects of the pastor's soul or skills, it commends the true work of ministry—shepherding, teaching, encouraging—while redefining what we mean by success in ministry.

978-0-8024-1619-3 | ALSO AVAILABLE AS AN EBOOK

Does the world make you dizzy?